Love Is the Healer

Love Is
the Healer

Stella Terrill Mann

Harper & Row, Publishers
New York, Evanston, San Francisco, London

Condensed versions of chapters 1 through 9 have appeared in *New* Magazine.

FIRST EDITION

Designed by Gwendolyn O. England

Library of Congress Cataloging in Publication Data

Mann, Stella Terrill.
  Love is the healer.
    1. Love (Theology) I. Title.
BV4639.M268   1974   248′.4   72-11359
ISBN 0-06-065415-5

Lovingly dedicated to the memory of my paternal grandparents,
Lewis Schellenger, Civil War veteran, member of the G.A.R.,
and Elizabeth Smith Schellenger.
The world is a better place because they lived.

Contents

Love Is the Healer

Message to the Reader

DON'T WAIT TILL TOMORROW!

If you need help ... heaven on earth ... the Man who overcame the world ... free-flowing energy ... the Son of Man ... the instant age ... experience pleasure, avoid pain ... black magic ... to move a mountain ... picture seeds ... plan of procedure ... expectation of good ... the way that works.

"He that believeth on me, the works that I do shall he do also; and greater works than these shall he do."

Jesus in John 14:12

WHEN PEOPLE COME TO ME for prayers and ask for help with their problems, I ask them: "Where does it hurt? What would it take to make you happy? What would you like to have changed? What is it you want me to pray about?"

Before I agree to accept them as students, they are required to take a large view of themselves as persons, to assess their known and hidden potentials, and to take a look at the world of tomorrow and the natural goal of the human race. They then decide whether they really want to work for soul growth and for increased self-consciousness which will lead them to social and cosmic consciousness and finally to Christ consciousness. They need to learn that life is a total, not just the immediate problem they have come to talk about.

To exist in today's world without a working idea of tomorrow is to rob ourselves of great good that could be ours right now. For what we think of tomorrow will affect every hour of our lives today.

History is filled with examples of the way of life that does not work. For nearly two thousand years the world has known the way that does work. It has not yet been fully tried. Today the world is at a crossroads. We can wreck our planet and ourselves or learn how to live within the law of love and build a heaven on earth.

For more than thirty years I have been working with people with problems and problem people and have seen such wonderful results in lives changed through a knowledge and use of the spiritual laws that I have become an incurable optimist about the outcome of the human race. We definitely can do something about our mistakes, threats, and problems. It is not a question of whether love will ever be used as a universal way of life, but only of how soon enough people will get together and build a better world through love put to work.

This is the age of the interim man. Like Moses, we have seen the Promised Land but have not been able to enter it because of our own past faults. But we are rapidly moving toward it. Slowly, at first, a few will make it. Others will follow. Finally, enough people will learn enough to do enough to build a heaven on earth. This will be a state of perfect harmony. The old world of inharmony, hatreds, ignorance, fears, poverty, and greed will pass away.

By tomorrow many people will have proved that we can do the works Jesus did and greater works. Today we have millions of so-called mentally ill people. I believe they are so spiritually sick that they have lost their way as normal human beings. Tomorrow there will be neither physical nor mental illness, no need to run and hide from life, and no pressures without that strength within cannot handle. Selfishness, greed, and hatred will have been cleared out of human consciousness. There will be no loneliness, no welfare, no prisons, and no broken families. No one will abuse a child or an animal, or pollute earth, his home. Sorrow will be almost unknown and of short duration.

Tomorrow there will be no hungry, unfed people. Every child will receive a good education which will include travel around the world to get to know other people. Trips to other planets will be as common then as air flights around the world today. All this good is coming because thousands of individuals will know how to use the natural power that fills all space, which Jesus knew and used at will. We look at the results of the use Jesus made of atomic and electronic power as miracles, which only he could do. He is the only person yet to come to earth who understood this natural power and how to use it. Jesus said, "I have overcome the world." He overcame the world consciousness of ignorance, fear, and false beliefs which lead to poverty, sickness, cruelty, and war. That same consciousness is holding man back today. But man can learn and use the truth that will set him free.

Jesus was aware of a natural power within himself with which he could contact, direct, and control the power locked up in every atom on earth and in space around us. Atoms are the building blocks of things. Jesus used this power so that the leprosy victim's flesh was instantly healed. He used this power to still the wind and waves of the sea, to find fish in the sea, to wither a fig tree, and to see a harvest at hand that was months away. He used that power within himself to direct power outside of himself to multiply cooked fish and loaves of baked bread in a basket by calling upon the free-flowing atoms to add themselves to the existing pattern to multiply. The free-flowing energy atoms had no choice but to obey.

Jesus is the only person yet to use the dominion over nature which Genesis declares is common to all men. He used it to put life back into the dead Lazarus and to command life to return to the widow's son and to the young girl. He further used it to change his own "dead" flesh to a shining new body that was made of such high energy that those at the tomb described it as "Light." Jesus warned them not to touch him. They, in flesh bodies, were of a different vibration. To have touched him might well have been harmful to him and to themselves. Later, Jesus developed a new body which they could see and which Thomas touched.

Using his authority to command the natural power in things, which scientist Sir James Jeans called "bottled up energy" and the rest of it, unseen, "free flowing energy," Jesus changed the water to wine and had meat to eat which no one else could see.

The good news is that you and I have this same power, which Jesus called the Father, within. He explained that he did what he saw the Father within do. He said any man could learn the spiritual laws and thus use the creative power God has given man. But before a man could use his authority over the things of the world, Jesus said, he would have to learn the law of love and live within it.

For nearly two thousand years the Christian world has worshiped Jesus from afar as the only begotten Son of God, as a divine being who therefore had powers that no mortal could have. But the Bible tells us that Jesus was the great example of what all men could be. Christians have not believed, have overlooked, or have been unwilling to pay the price of such use of their power over atomic energy. After the early centuries the Christian Church gave up healing because it demanded too much self-discipline and love. Today many Christians still ask Jesus, the Christ-consciousness Man, to do for them what he taught that all men can do for themselves. He died to prove his words.

Scientist Lecomte du Noüy says that Jesus, who called himself the Son of Man, is the pattern of what all men will be eventually. According to du Noüy, Jesus was a million years ahead of today's man. But in his great book, *Human Destiny*, he makes no mention of the New Thought movement, whose Christian members do believe that man has the power Jesus had. This is part of the truth they teach and try to live up to. The reader can learn about this movement in *Spirits in Rebellion: The Rise And Development of New Thought*, by the historian Charles S. Braden. The movement is now about one hundred years old.

Some people are frightened by the idea that they have the same power that Jesus had to heal the sick through the power of their word. They fear that only evil could come from such dominion over nature. We need to look carefully into this point. Before God, the Creator of the universe, could grant to man the use of such power, He had to have a way to keep man from wrongly using the power and so destroying others and himself. To understand what this method is and how it works puts us on our knees in awe, wonder, and gratitude for the greatness of God and the depths of His love for man, who already is only "a little lower than the angels" and destined to become as a god.

Using the power within him, man can indeed become as a devil as well as a god. The unbreakable law of safety is that *man cannot use this power within until he has become a complete love person.*

A love person can and does create good, and only good, as does God. As Jesus stated, man can do what he sees the Father within doing. Man is a child of God but will not reach his spiritual maturity as a son of God until he has become a complete love person. When he does reach that maturity, he will work directly with the power Jesus knew and used. Man's need is not to beg God for more good, health, wealth, and happiness, but to learn to so live within the spiritual laws that his creative power will instantly produce for him as it did for Jesus. Wide use of this power will take man into the instant age, a far cry from the stone age. From the first, man was destined to grow. I believe that many now living will achieve Christ consciousness.

Psychologists and psychiatrists say it is infantile to want good instantly. I cannot agree. I think the infant may come inwardly equipped with a desire for instant satisfactions so that he will, during his lifetime, work to learn how to perform tasks at will, as Jesus did. Earth is a school where man is sent to learn how to use his free will in such a way that he harms no one, not even himself. To do this, he must learn the spiritual laws, especially the highest of them all—the law of love. For when he lives within it, all the things he needs and wants can be added to him by the power of his word. He will do the works that Jesus did and greater, for as the world advances, new and greater needs arise.

Infants as well as adults want to experience pleasure and avoid pain. If the growing child is allowed to avoid the responsibility of his freewill acts, he will remain a spiritual infant and not mature into the stage of using the Christ power within himself.

The life and teachings of Jesus tell us that the use of our God-given power is foolproof. It must be used for good and only good, or it simply does not obey man's will. Many attempt to use the creative power of mind outside of the law of love. History long has called this practice black magic. But it rebounds and harms the user. Such people have been known to destroy themselves in expiation for their sense of guilt. We see this happening in lesser degree in people all around us, which accounts for much physical and mental illness. Before we can do the things Jesus did, we must become the kind of love person that Jesus was.

Today man uses the reverse of the creative power Jesus used. Man has gone to great pains to *split the atom*, to release the energy in it. Scientists have shown that if they can release the power in the atoms, man will build a paradise on earth. Food will be dirt cheap, they already are telling us. And war will be no more, with no need for conquest of land, goods, or gold.

Modern science says that space is charged with energies, which mean raw power, that would transform the earth if we knew how to release and control them. Sir Oliver Lodge said that a single cubic inch of ether—that space "out there"—contains energy enough to run a forty-horsepower engine forty million years! Man will harness that energy and fly his planes with it, run his machinery with it, and end all pollution and poverty. Man has been going at this problem of energy on the lowest level—physical and material. But by using a higher level of force, his own thought, to direct a spiritual power, *he can command that raw energy to do his bidding*. Does this seem like a science-fiction dream? Well, Jesus said that a man could move a mountain if he had faith. But his whole ministry of teaching and demonstrating the use of such power showed that we cannot have faith until we first have love. Jesus proved that any infraction of the law of love weakens our faith to that degree, and that acts of love build faith. Our faith, in turn, strengthens love. Energy works in a circle.

Mind working without love is destructive. Mind working with love is creative. According to the old idea of good and evil, there are two powers: one of them evil, a devil, able to overcome God, or good, and winning much too often. Tomorrow we shall see that it is one and the same power, which can be used for good or evil. Evil cannot create good. It can only destroy. But evil is limited in how far it can destroy. It can destroy on the mental plane and make people ill or drive them insane. It can destroy on the spiritual plane, as immoral people prove. But it cannot destroy life itself. It can but harm the house life temporarily inhabits.

By tomorrow millions will have learned so to live within the law of love that they will be using the power within themselves to control, to use at will both the free atoms in space to create new things, and the bottled-up atoms, as in blindness, cancer, and calcium deposits that cause arthritis. Food plants will be made to develop from seed to harvest. Men will *plant seed ideas, picture seeds* of what they need, and command the free energy atoms to assemble themselves in the framework; just as today, bees come and fill in the honeycomb man provides in the man-made hive. The miracles of Jesus were not the result of breaking known laws, but of working within laws not yet fully known to man. Our need is first to learn the spiritual laws and live within them, and then all else will develop naturally.

Life on earth ought to be easier, happier, and more joyful and abundant for everyone than it ever has been for anyone. Jesus said that he came "that they might have my joy fulfilled in themselves" (John 17:13). *Webster's Third New International Dictionary* defines joy as "the emotion excited by the acquisition or expectation of good; gladness, delight." Jesus had great joy because he knew he had great power and that man was not helpless before circumstances. This was his great good news: "Any man can do what I have done."

But nature leaves no gaps. We must learn the laws. Law flows down from principle. A principle cannot be broken. Laws can be broken or denied. Love is the principle of life, and the laws of love flow down from this principle. Hence Jesus gave the two great commandments for the only safe and happy way to live, the only method that leads to progressive good for man. "Thou shalt love the Lord thy God with all thy heart, and with all thy soul and with all thy mind. This is the first and great commandment. And the second is like unto it, Thou shalt love thy neighbor as thyself." And further: "On these two commandments hang all the law and the prophets." These words of Jesus (Matt. 22:37–40) will yet be the law of the world.

The teachings of Jesus were not completely original with him, of course. He was well-grounded in the Hebrew Bible. There we read, "Thou shalt also decree a thing, and it shall be established unto thee; and the light shall shine upon thy ways" (Job 22:28). And also: "Death and life are in the power of the tongue" (Prov. 18:21). Doctors today tell us that many people do talk themselves into sickness and death. Scientists have shown that human beings can, by the power of their word and emotions, wither living plants, as Jesus withered the fig tree.

For ages man has been told that he has the power of the Father within, by whatever name it has been called. But Jesus was the first man to grasp the reasons back of the two great commandments, the first to break through cosmic consciousness to Christ consciousness, the first to declare that all men have this power in potential. But man always is slow to accept his good. The early Greeks knew that the earth is a sphere. But it took two thousand more years for men to accept and use that fact for their continued progress.

Just before the crucifixion Jesus told his disciples, "I will pray the Father and he shall give you [all mankind] another Comforter." Later, he spelled out what he meant by Comforter: "When he, the Spirit of truth, is come he will guide you into all truth." (John 14:16; 16:13.)

Jesus used the power of the Word, which is a masculine and projective power, to impregnate the World Soul, which is feminine and receptive, with the Spirit of truth, also a masculine and mental power. This impregnation gave birth to the age of truth. We are still in the age of truth and new ideas, dreams, accomplishments, discoveries, demands, changes, and facts will come in faster and faster as this age goes on toward the year two thousand.

The meek shall inherit the earth. The meek are the teachable people, those who want to learn and will take the time and make the effort to do so. Tomorrow's better world, that heaven on earth, will be brought in and maintained by the people who have learned first to rule their own spirits. The spirit is the intent and purpose of (the will of) *the soul self,* which is my term for the human personality. The spirit dictates the feelings, emotions, thoughts, words, deeds, and methods of accomplishing its desires. This is why the Old Testament tells us to "train the child up," meaning into higher consciousness.

When people come to me for help, I set up a program for accomplishment and a method of procedure that will daily guide them toward their desired goal. This book was written to share with my readers the methods I long have used in working with individuals who sincerely want to change their lives for the better. It is designed for the reader to follow at his own pace after he learns the principles. It is based entirely on the two great love commandments of Jesus and covers the eighteen points of the law of love given and implied in the commandments and in the other teachings of Jesus.

Part one of the book starts out simply, using case histories from my files showing how students learned one point of the law at a time. In the first nine chapters, the reader sees how my students learned to become soul-self-conscious. In part two, the reader begins to work for social and cosmic consciousness. At the end of the book there is a three-part test to enable the reader to evaluate his progress. There is nothing difficult in the process of learning if we take one point at a time and see how it leads logically to the next point. From our first lesson, I tell my students, "Don't wait till tomorrow! Start today to build a new and better life for yourself." And to the reader I say, "Start now to learn how to live within the law of love and to receive the good that can be yours today."

STELLA TERRILL MANN

Pasadena, California

PART ONE

Soul–Self–Consciousness

To build your soul-self-consciousness, build a house of love. A house of love is made up of nine points of love. Happiness dwells where spiritually mature, whole people live. A whole, spiritually mature person is one who has developed both sides of his nature: the mind, or masculine side, and the soul, or feminine side. The mature person does not think of masculine and feminine only as a difference in sex, but also in spirit. The whole person respects and takes care of his physical body as the place where the living soul presently dwells.

"If we analyze our motives we will find
[that they are] made either of love or of fear."

Emerson

1 Love: The Healer of Loneliness

LOVE YOURSELF

*Happiness lives in a house of love . . . definitions of love . . .
love of self builds an eastern wall . . . love always listens . . .
be a nice person to know . . . knowledge is power if . . . love
leads to work or action.*

Story from Life: The Young Woman Who Cried Her Eyes In

"Thou shalt love . . . thyself."
Jesus in Matthew 22:39

WE ALL WANT HAPPINESS, joy in living, a sense of satisfaction, and
a complete fulfillment in life. The desire for happiness is instinctive, deeper than reason and far more compelling. Unhappiness
is nature's way of warning us that something is wrong in our lives
that, if not righted, can lead to sickness and even to death, as
statistics show.

It is a mistake to think that a certain person, place, or thing will
give us happiness. Happiness results from many needs being met
in the right way, and the greatest of these needs is love. Our need
for love includes having our love accepted, finding a home and
welcome that invite us to visit there often and that send love back
to us in return. Only then can the divine energy of love complete
its circuit from God, through us, and back to God.

When people come to me for help and prayers, no matter what
the problem seems to be, I quickly learn about their love quo-
tient. My search begins with the first need, love of self. As a
religious practitioner and teacher of the spiritual laws, I find few
who understand the grim necessity of self-love, much less how to
achieve it. They have been taught that self-love is unchristian,
selfish, sinful—bad.

But in the abbreviated Bible passage at the beginning of this chapter, part of the two great commandments, Jesus pointed out a fact about love which has been overlooked for centuries and still is largely overlooked today. It is this: *We must first love ourselves before we can hope to love our neighbor.*

It is psychologically impossible to know how to love a wife, husband, or child, let alone a neighbor, until we first love ourselves. Jesus knew that self-love has to do with soul value; hence his commandment. Happiness is impossible to the individual who does not have self-respect, self-reliance, and self-approval. Psychologists speak of self-acceptance as part of the survival pattern. Since example is still the best teacher, let me tell you about Janet,* *the young woman who cried her eyes in.*

When Janet phoned me she had read one of my books and wanted to come for prayers. I asked, "What is your problem?"

"I'm sick of everything and see no way to change things. I work all day and stay home evenings and cry my eyes out."

"Then you need to learn how to cry them in again," I said, and we set a date.

Janet was prompt for her appointment. From her life history, which I took at the time, the following points are of interest here: Janet, thirty years old, had never married and had had no dates with young men since high school. Twenty pounds overweight, she dressed unbecomingly, tortured rather than dressed her blond hair, had an attitude of sad hopelessness, looked down at her red, rough hands when she talked, and seemed unable to get her words out over her teeth. She had beautiful blue eyes, held a good job at a bank, and was an efficient, loyal employee.

Janet's parents were divorced when she was a baby. Her mother was then in her fourth unhappy marriage. At the time she came to me for counseling, Janet lived alone in an apartment where she "could cook the food she liked, listen to good music, and cry alone." She attended church now and then, but made no friends.

* Here and elsewhere names have been changed to ensure the personal anonymity of those whose cases are discussed.

When we got through with her history, I said, "What is it you want to pray about?"

Janet pushed her hands out in front of her and said, "I want to get rid of this ugly eczema forever. It comes and goes. Sometimes it is so bad I scratch it until it bleeds. The doctor can't seem to keep it away."

"Of course he can't," I said and took a clipping from my resource file of a report Dr. O. C. Spurgeon English of Temple Medical School made to the American Academy of Dermatology and Syphilology concerning eczema. He said, "The patients are usually depressed and long for love. . . . Eczema patients subjected to stress have a longing for a soothing hand. The hand which scratches is the soothing hand, temporarily, at least. The patient cannot weep, but his skin weeps for him."

"My skin is crying because I want to and can't, like at work?" Janet asked, puzzled.

"When stress comes into your life, possibly in your work, you begin to realize that you are alone, and have no man with a shoulder to cry on." Janet started to snivel but I went on: "There is nothing else in your personal history to make you cry your eyes out. Let's face the hidden reason: you want just what you should want, love, a husband, home, children—happiness. When you take care of your happiness, your happiness will take care of that weeping skin. If you want a love of your own, you will have to admit it and ask for it."

After more talk Janet said, "Yes, I do want a love of my own, a happy marriage, children, before it is too late. Not all husbands run away. I see lots of happily married young women. I envy them. I don't want a man just to cry on his shoulder, but to do things with and for."

"Your purpose is correct. You start by becoming good marriage material. First, you learn to love yourself—"

"I can't," Janet broke in. "I'm so ugly; have crooked teeth; hate myself for hating Mother because she didn't have them fixed when I was young. Hate myself because I don't know how to make friends. Hate myself for hating my father because he ran away—"

"Hate is a defense against fear," I said. "If you loved yourself, neither the crooked teeth nor the mistakes of your parents would bother you now. And you'd know how to make friends. *Until you love yourself* you cannot hope to draw a worthwhile young man to you. Because what you think about yourself goes out from you to others. They believe about you what you believe about yourself. So first, you must have self-approval. You will then draw to yourself both men and women who are in your natural orbit. This has to happen, because the laws of attraction and repulsion, of sowing and reaping, are ever alive and working. We can't turn them off but we can use them for our needs and purposes."

"Where do I start?" Janet asked, eager and determined.

"By understanding something about the law of love itself. There are many definitions of love. The one you need now is this: *Love is the power that makes an intelligent response to the needs of the object of its affection.*"

I explained to Janet my method of helping students to build a good self-consciousness by building a house of love where happiness will take up permanent residence and make of it a home. This means building the soul, personality, consciousness, body, mind, and spirit. The soul, says Webster, means, "man's moral and emotional nature . . . a seat of real life, vitality, or action . . . a vital principle actuating something . . . moving spirit . . . leader."

The student also looks at other meanings: that self of us which was created by God, that which is deathless in us, destined to live forever. Our entity, beingness, which makes us different from all other beings on earth. That part of us which we call a living soul and a child of God.

Janet's first need was to build an eastern wall for her house of love, which means to build the right kind of self-love. She was advised to make some intelligent responses to her physical, mental, and spiritual needs, to reduce her weight, to learn about clothes and hair styles, to swim and to dance. Janet also needed to think well of herself, to forgive all childhood hurts, and to learn the art and science of feeling and expressing love.

As I listed some of her good qualities, Janet copied them down. She had fitted herself to work and earn; she remained moral and decent in spite of loneliness. She was kind to her mother, though she did not like being with her.

Honest by nature and intent, Janet did not lie, cheat, or steal. She valued her life and the lives of others, and drove her car carefully. She valued the time of others and had come on time for her appointment. She had proved her love of learning and respect for wisdom by wanting to study. There were other points. When I had done, Janet had a most impressive picture of her worth.

"You do care about yourself," I said. "You would not have survived if you had not cared enough to make right decisions, to take right advantages. Now *you need to be conscious of your own worth and to get others to be aware of it also.*"

We went into my room with the tall double mirrors, where my students learn how to evaluate what they see in themselves. Placing her before the mirrors I said, among other directives, "Smile in such a way that you compliment the beholder. Make your smile say: 'You are a nice person. You please me.' "

Janet looked down at her hands and clammed up.

"Even in a bank a smile is worth its face value," I reminded her.

Janet's mouth stretched a bit, but she couldn't smile. When I said, "Smile in such a way that you tell me what a wonderful person you are, and worth knowing," Janet started to snivel again and said it would be dishonest, she did not want to wear her heart on her sleeve, flirting like her mother to try to catch a man.

"You don't wear your heart on your sleeve when you smile; you wear it on your face and in your eyes and attitude," I said.

Before Janet left that day we had worked up a smile for her which she was to improve upon by practicing in front of her mirror with *thought and feeling.* She was to go into the bank every morning trailing an invisible cloud of love, happiness, and even mystery with her. "You don't have to do anything," I reminded her. "You just have to *think, feel and believe* that there are wonderful people all around you who want to be your friends, and who also need a friend. You are a child of God. Be proud of it! The people you meet are also children of God, your kinfolks, worthy of your notice and praise. And a smile is a curve that can set a lot of things straight."

Janet was daily to:

> Put love in your eyes
> Like the light in the skies;
> Put love in your words,
> Like the song of the birds:
> Put love in your mind,
> And a true love you'll find.

This would happen because the law of attraction and repulsion would work for Janet to bring love to her, but it would then be up to her to hold or to lose it. She would have to learn how to become happily involved with other people, which would be "loving out."

Right then, Janet needed to learn how to cry her eyes in. "You have been using the wrong method of crying," I said. Opening the dictionary I read, "To cry is 'to lament audibly; to weep.' That is what you have been doing. To cry also means 'to make a loud sound, as in prayer, also entreaty; appeal.' Now to make the right kind of appeal, in prayer, for the right kind of help will be to cry your eyes in."

Janet's daily prayer was: "*Let the Spirit of love dry my tears, still my fears, arrange my affairs, and bring to me a love of my own.*" Janet learned about the term "Spirit of love." The spirit of anything is the intent and purpose of it. Love is caring with all the fervor of which the heart is capable. *Love is the nature of God in action.*

Since Janet was to believe that the Spirit of love, alive and working in the universe, could do exactly as she asked in prayer and lived up to, she stated boldly with me that her prayer already had been done, in spirit, in *idea form*. Properly understood, this is exactly what Jesus taught. It is the law of faith: believe–receive.

Reporting to me often, Janet worked faithfully in prayer, dieting, swimming, and dancing. Her skin cleared quickly. Pounds melted away. With hope and a plan of procedure, Janet was happier and busier than ever before in her life. She had fun, met new people, and was alone only when she wanted to be. No more tears in the night. Through group activities she met a few men, but not *the* man. When her faith wavered I reminded her: "Love will never let you down if you will hold it up for all to see."

Nightly, Janet asked herself: "Did I grow today?" Building an eastern wall of self-love takes growing by doing, thinking, and feeling. It was not easy. Her mother came and wanted to run Janet's life after she had pretty well ruined her own with possessive love. Janet called on the Spirit of love for help and handled the situation without hurt to either of them.

About one year passed while Janet steadily gained in poise, self-respect, and love of others. "I have a good chance to practice my smile and interest in people," she told me. "Strangers come to my desk all day long."

And one day *the* man walked in. His business brought him to Janet's desk. He was a tall, towering, gruff kind of man. "What have you got to smile about?" he asked Janet, looking straight into her beautiful blue eyes.

"It would take a long time to tell you, sir," Janet said and smiled.

"I have the time to spare," said the young man, "and I want to learn." He handed Janet his card and continued, "I'm single, honest, have a good reputation with my company. You can check up on me."

"Well," said Janet, smiling, "that's a refreshing approach. You must be a very different and interesting person."

"I am," said the young man. "How about dinner with me Saturday night? We can go to a show later, if you'd like."

Janet looked at his card, recognized the business house that banked there, noted this young man had a title with that company, and her old fears rose up. She could not speak.

"Are you afraid of me?" the man asked gruffly.

"No," said Janet, remembering he was a child of God and kinfolk. "I know a gentleman when I see one."

The date was set for that Saturday night. Janet rushed to me after work, stars in her eyes, fear in her voice. What should she wear? What should she talk about?

"Don't talk," I advised. "*Love always listens. Let him talk!* Listen, and smile your approval of his charming and stimulating company. Really listen, and you'll learn whether he is an honest, lonely man as you think, or a wolf in an expensive and well-fitting suit. Everybody needs somebody; what kind of people does he need? Is he marriage material? He will tell you the truth about himself if you just sit entranced and *listen.* Honestly and generously care about him as a human being; offer genuine sympathy, interest, and friendly companionship. If you feel it, he will know it and react to it. He wants to know what kind of person you are, too. Be your best self. Remember your own worth. Above all, *listen with love.* We expect God to listen to our prayers. Every lonely person is praying for someone to listen without criticism."

So Janet went on her date to learn about becoming involved with other people. Later she told me about it: "Like him . . . think he likes me . . . he's thirty-six, never married. Took care of his mother, sent his kid brother through school after his father died. Mother died last year. Likes same music I do. Thinks his nose is ugly. Told him it is unusual and interesting. Hates his first name, uses initial, D, only. Told him it meant dignity to me." And on and on.

After several happy dates with D, Janet struck an all-time low. What if he didn't ever come to love her? "You are not running this show alone," I reminded her. "You asked the Spirit of love to do the work. Spirit never stops short of the completion of its work. But it does not usurp your free will. It will help you if you ask, but then *you must let it.* Doubts and fears stop the good work. To believe is to receive, good, bad, or indifferent. So believe the good that you do want to receive is coming straight to you."

When D wanted Janet to meet his uncle and family, Janet, slim and very attractive with the joy of living, brought her new blue dress to show me. "Be sure to wear your smile too," I warned. She must have. For D reported that his uncle and family liked Janet very much. Then Janet brought her young man to meet me, and he took us both out to dinner. I told Janet I thought the D in his first name meant desirable and dependable, and that he was good marriage material and was obviously looking for a wife. I told her that his gruff manner was due to embarrassment at not having had a lot of girls in his life. "And I think he is in love with you," I added.

When Janet showed me her engagement ring I told her that the light in her eyes truly outshone the diamond in her ring.

At the prewedding party D's uncle gave for the happy couple, I watched Janet in action. Her smile said, "I'm a nice person to know. I love people. I am interested in you. Tell me about yourself." This was the Spirit of love at work, not cheap pretending. It was real, both an art and a science. It was communication by unspoken thoughts and feelings. Under the law of likeness it set up a benevolent circle of love around Janet and the other person, who then put forth his best efforts at being what she made him feel he was. Janet had learned to project what she had become.

Watching Janet, I realized that before these two young people met, each thought something was wrong with himself. But the Spirit of love found them both to be acceptable, and they found themselves to be acceptable to each other. Oh yes, they married. And did they live happily ever after? They had problems, adjustments to make, but they knew what to do. They studied all the points of love discussed in this book. Each respected himself and the other; they both wanted their marriage to last. Their home in turn became the center for happy and growing young couples.

Some of the laws Janet learned and consciously applied to her personal life were the laws of cause and effect, sowing and reaping, and Ampère's theory of electrical magnetism which states that parallel currents in the same direction attract one another, and parallel currents in opposite directions repel one another. The need is to learn these laws and work with them for a definite purpose. But knowledge is power only if used. Our purpose here is to reach through to a radiant, happy, useful, and satisfying way of life which harms no one and blesses all it touches.

So that we may work together as we go on, let me explain why we take a student's case history and the mirror test.

1. *The unexamined life is hardly worth living*

My questions to the student, "Where are you going? Where does it hurt?" show me where he has been in life experiences, where he presently stands, in which direction he is headed, and what he is doing for or against himself. His infractions against the law of love are clearly shown as his story unfolds.

2. *Why we learn the love quotient*

The ideal is for the child to be born into a home of love and be adjusted, ready to meet others and life beyond the walls of his own home, by the time he starts school. But not all children are so fortunate. I have learned I must work with the student where he presently stands in his ability to give and to receive love.

3. *Why we take the mirror test*

It is necessary to let the student see for himself what his thoughts and emotions of the past have done to his physical body. He must learn to recognize both the good and bad, the desirable and undesirable traits of character which show up in body, mind, and spirit. The student needs to look for hidden potentials in his total soul-mind-self. In the very unhappy person the good potentials are nearly always overlooked. In the very fearful person they appear impossible to attain. But even bad habits can reveal good potentials.

4. *All growing people can benefit by the mirror test*

I began the mirror test after watching women buy clothing in a department store. As they stood before a full-length mirror, the changes in their expressions as they viewed themselves in the new dresses was startling. It was obvious th it they were taking a critical look at their inside selves. Their manner and changing expressions were saying, "I used to be more attractive." They picked at their hair, patted at their faces, pulled their shoulders up. What they saw in the mirror did not live up to the new garments they would wear.

We all know we could be more physically attractive, have better health, and be happier persons every day of our lives. Few people are satisfied with themselves or their accomplishments, the braggart least of all. The more satisfied we are with ourselves, the easier it is for us to become happily involved with others and meaningfully involved with life.

The daily mirror test will help us to see many parts of the truth about ourselves—where we have been, where we stand, where it hurts, what we want changed, and what it would take to make us happy. But best of all, we will begin to *see how far ahead we could go.*

Children love the mirror test. "There are nine of me," said a little boy of the reflected and re-reflected images of himself, "and they are all laughing." I strongly recommend this inexpensive aid to self-betterment for the family. It helps a child to establish his identity and helps adults to watch their improvement as their learning proceeds. The daily mirror test and inventory can give the student great joy.

5. *Use of affirmations*

My students are required to use affirmations as well as prayer. Affirmations say something is so, and they are accepted by the subconscious mind which begins to act on the truth stated. Many of the prayers and affirmations which I create for my students are written rhymes or jingles, because the conscious mind learns them quickly and has pleasure in using them. The reader will do well to create his own affirmations and prayers in verse or rhymes. Every time he says, for example, "I Love God and God loves me, and we are a wonderful team, you see," it becomes more true to him. Life becomes easier and happier, for he has his subconscious working for him with that truth. It is like earning interest on saved money.

The test for feelings of love is this: *does it do anything?* If it is love, it goes into action to make things better in some way. It seeks to promote the highest welfare of the object of its affection, be it a person, thing, or principle, such as beauty, truth, justice, harmony, freedom, peace, or whatever good merits promotion, protection, and presentation. *Work always follows feelings of love.* The work of love always leads toward more freedom for the individual and for mankind.

We have started out simply in these lessons, but before we are through we will have touched the heights of the goals of humanity and of our present world problems that seem to hold back some of the good we want right now. If we understand each lesson in turn, we will be just as sure of success in the final lesson as we are in this first one. Why delay success? Let us go on with our next lesson and continue to build our house of love.

2 Love: The Healer of Poverty

LOVE OTHERS

*Work is the teacher . . . poverty is no picnic . . . love others
. . . love can multiply money . . . praise and raise people up
. . . keep an open-end mind . . . check your plans and
specifications . . . work leads to decisions.*

Story from Life: The Man Who Turned His Bread to Stones

"Thou shalt love thy neighbor."

Jesus in Matthew 22:39

THIS BOOK IS DESIGNED to help the individual to learn the spiritual laws through working with them. We are building a house of love, our soul-self, and along with it, constantly raising the level of our consciousness. Our objective is a good, useful, and happy life. Happiness is made up of many needs rightly met. The greatest of these needs is love, which has many parts. In this chapter we want to see how love multiplies money.

Love gives. And if a man who is honest and honorable fails to provide for his family and himself, he is affected adversely in body, mind, and spirit. Poverty is no picnic. Poverty is the result of breaking the law of love somewhere along the line. For example, let me tell you about Henry, *the man who turned his bread to stones.*

When Henry phoned me for an appointment I asked, "What is your problem?"

"No problem but money," he replied crisply.

"That can't be entirely true," I said, "for if there were no other problems, there would be money with enough to spare. We need to learn what is keeping money away."

When Henry came we sat out in the patio which faces east

toward my garden of trees: lemon, Rangpur lime, tangerine, kumquat, orange, Santa Rosa plum, maple, and others. I keep the ground bare so the birds can dust their feathers and rest in the shade. That morning, the cautious doves and sassy blue jays came and went from the dripping water basin. Pink oleanders, orchid crepe myrtle, red geraniums, white lilies, and other flowers bloomed gaily, as if singing a song of gratitude to Mother Nature. Far over to the north, Mount Wilson stood in majestic guard over all of the broad San Gabriel Valley. The sun poured forth light and energy. But all that display of happy Mother Nature and all-providing Father God was lost on Henry. He was too conscious of his immediate problems.

"Lately, everything I eat gives me trouble," he said. "Feels like rocks in my stomach." He poured a glass of water, took some white pills, and settled himself to tell me his story.

Henry, thirty-eight, had a wife and three sons whom he loved devotedly. He worked for a store that sold paint, hardware, and other building materials. He was a skilled mechanic generally and an expert in certain building-industry fields.

The crisis that brought him to me was a fear he would lose his job. He had quarreled with "Old Gridley," owner of the store, who was preparing to vacation in Europe with his wife. "He will keep me while he is gone," Henry said unhappily, "but he will fire me when he returns and can replace me."

The quarrel had resulted from Henry's bitterly criticizing Gridley over handling an account. "It amounts to cheating," Henry had accused Gridley. "You should have told the man there was another brand of paint that costs less; what you sold him was too expensive for the cheap job he's doing."

"We sell what the customer asks for," Gridley hotly replied. "Leave the moralizing to the church; our business is to make money!"

More remarks of that kind had followed, Henry glumly admitted.

When I asked Henry what he wanted me to pray for, he said, "Enough money so that I can go into business for myself. I want to teach my boys to be honest men, the best in the building trade."

Henry went into a long recital of "what is wrong with our country," from government interference with business, labor-union tactics, taxes "paid for by honest, hardworking men who are trying to hold things together." Henry had much to say about "the staggering increase of the welfare load, and the government's giveaway programs." He ended with, "And the modern boy does not see enough of his father. I want my kids with me every day, being trained from the minute they get out of school."

"A builder of men is a good idea, a 'God idea,'" I said. "Why haven't you put it into effect?"

When Henry had finished telling me the story of his life, we went into the house for the mirror test. I explained why we use it. Henry stood ramrod straight in front of the mirror; arms folded across his chest; every muscle in his face tight; his mouth a straight line. He wore a blue sport shirt, open at the neck, short sleeves, and clean blue jeans—a workingman's clothes.

"What do you see that you don't like about yourself," I asked.

"Nothing," Henry replied, a little on the defensive.

"What do you feel about yourself that you don't like?"

Henry's body relaxed; his arms dropped to his sides. "I'm sick of being poor. My brother-in-law earns three times as much as I do, but I know I'm smarter than he is. I'm ashamed."

All of Henry's shames had to do with not having enough money to buy the things and opportunities he wanted for his family and himself. I told Henry that he could take pride in being ashamed of being poor; that God had provided abundance for all; that he had a right and a high duty to ask for more as long as he lived. But that he must keep strictly within the law of love to obtain it. "You want more money. We must start with what you have in hand. What are you worth right now?"

Henry told me his salary and added, "Broke and in debt, paying on a home, just about keeping up with current bills."

"Is there anything wrong with your right hand?" I asked.

Henry looked startled, stretched the hand out before him, and said, "No, why did you ask?"

"If you lost it in an accident—if you couldn't drive nails, or saw wood, how much would you want from an insurance company in compensation?"

Henry closed his eyes and stood very still. Then he said, "I'm following through with you, Mrs. Mann. I also have a perfect left hand, two perfect eyes—don't even wear glasses—two perfect ears and feet. I guess," Henry paused, tears in his voice, "it's just my head. I get so damned mad at people! I bawl them out. They don't do their work right. I'm a misfit. I belong to the days when an individual earned a living by the excellence of his work and took pride in it." He opened his eyes and glared at me and said, "And, by God, I'm right about it!"

"Look at yourself again," I said, "and tell yourself this: 'Henry, you are too rich to be standing here, making a poor mouth. Man, you are worth a million dollars on the hoof.'"

Henry gulped, but haltingly said it. Then we went into my office and started to work on his problem.

First, about the rocks in his stomach, "You are turning your bread to stones," I said. "The bread of life for every man is his free will, his ability to decide what he will think, feel, refuse, accept, and do. You choose the thoughts you will eat—accept, or take in—and so *learn how to eat the bread of life and turn the stones to bread.* You do this by learning how to work consciously and willingly with the Spirit of love. Choose only the good, God, and the love way of life."

I told Henry some of the meanings of love: love is caring about with all the fervor of which the heart is capable. Love is God in action. Love is good desires without fear. A good desire with fear is an idle wish, a daydream, or a nightmare of indecision, a distortion and not a plan. Henry needed to neutralize his feelings of fear and failure and to stabilize his feelings of desire for greater good for his family and himself. He needed to build a house of love and to start with the four walls.

"Ought to begin with a foundation," Henry interrupted stubbornly, with authority.

"No, you begin with *desire*, and then go on to *decision* and action. You must first have proper plans and specifications prepared," I corrected and added, "My housing project is a visual education method I created to teach ordinary people like myself the way of life that works. It brings abstract facts into concrete pictures. It takes the wear, tear, and swear out of daily living."

Henry's blue eyes sought my face, fearing he had offended me. There could be no teaching until we were on level ground again. I smiled reassuringly and said, "Henry, technically you are correct about actual building. The foundation must go down first. In the ideal family the child gets the four footings of his life foundation all set before he reaches school age. And especially if he belongs to a large family with relatives who do much visiting. Then in life he continues to grow and builds the four walls of his house of love, safely anchored to the ideal foundation. By the time he is ready for marriage, he has a house of love completed. He is a mature soul-self, ready to share his self with another mature soul-self. But your life story showed me that you did not have that kind of childhood. We must start right where you stand. Ready to listen?"

"Yes ma'am," Henry said, relieved. "But first, I want to say that you've made me see that I'm making the same mistake with my kids that my parents made with me and my wife's parents made with her."

After understanding that in my system of picturing an eastern wall means "love the self," Henry agreed that he was a good and honest man, that he loved and respected himself. "Love has no tricks," I said. "Love wears an open face. Its intent and purpose are always apparent. Love of justice, goodness, and honesty show through you."

But there were areas in which Henry did not approve of himself. For example: he was long on ethics and morals, short on love of others. Part of his criticism about shoddy work today was justified, but he was also trying to make himself feel superior, explaining why others made money and he didn't. Together we got it all straight. Henry saw that you don't have to be dishonest to make money. He needed a southern wall for his house of love—to love others. He admitted that he did no public services and no volunteer work for a better community, church, or country. His circle of love was very small—his family and himself.

I gave Henry this definition of love to work with: *Love is what you feel that makes you do things for certain people for free that you wouldn't do for anyone else for money.* He finally saw that he had that kind of love only for his family and that he needed to have it for others if he was to succeed in life.

Henry was to repeat as his daily prayer:

> Let the Spirit of love heal all my ills,
> Pay all my bills,
> Work through my talents and desires,
> And show me the way to make them pay.

The opportunity to serve others would come, and when Henry had accepted it in his consciousness, the money would follow. Henry needed to love others, and to show them that he did in such a way that his love would be accepted and returned in kind. This would set up a benevolent *circle of living love, the most powerful force known to man.* Henry was quick to learn the rules when I compared the power of love to the power of electricity.

"Through me . . . I use it . . . as the electric power turns the wheel, lights the globe, goes back to the powerhouse all in an instant. Ought to work," Henry agreed thoughtfully.

"It will work if you will let it," I assured him. "Jesus knew how to use this power and got instant results. God does not usurp our free will. And when enough people in the world learn the laws of love and privately live within them, we will no longer have the public problems you were worrying about. You can't reform the world nor your boss. But the ninety-first Psalm tells how and why you, as an individual, can go through, now, no matter what the rest of the world is doing. Study that Psalm."

Of himself Henry said, "I'm D.C. current—direct critic in that electricity love bit. I do it to their faces and sometimes quite fluently."

"And you sometimes enjoy it," I added.

"Every time," Henry admitted, avoiding my eyes.

"Part of building that southern wall, love of others, is to give a tithe of your time and money. It can be as little as you desire, to start." I told Henry of the Unity School of Christianity money blessing: "Divine Love, through me, blesses and multiplies this love offering." And to add to it as I do: ". . . tenfold, to the giver and to the receiver, that the law of abundance may be kept. Let this money go out and bless every hand it touches and quicken the mind of the receiver to the fact that there is plenty for all and to spare. Let the law of abundance be kept." *In the law of tithing we give with no strings attached.* But we can rightfully speak the word for unending increase.

In his work, as he used the yardstick and tape measure, Henry was to remember that the golden rule for human conduct never has been improved upon for human relations and wealth. All of our man-made laws that try to force honesty, fairness, justice, and responsibility are but confessions that the golden rule is the way to wealth.

We need to study the meaning of the golden rule if we desire to earn money. In the command, "Whatsoever ye would that men should do to you, do ye even so to them" (Matt. 7:12), we see that Jesus recognized free will. His rule presumes that a man can grow to that point of goodness where nothing can hold him back but himself. This is a truth about human life on earth. Some five hundred years before Christ, the Chinese philosopher Confucius stated the rule in a negative manner: "Do not do unto others what you do not want them to do to you." That was Henry's actual use of the rule. But merely to refrain from harming others is not enough for the growth of one's own soul, nor is it enough to build a monetary fortune, nor enough to build a better world for all people. *To love is to act.* Jesus, the Christ-consciousness Man, saw and taught this fact. In his great commandment he made it clear: *love others.* All his works and teaching proved his positive statement: do unto others. *Love always goes to work.* This Henry needed to learn and put into daily practice.

Henry had found it difficult to "say complimentary things to people."

"Then practice on your dog," I said. "Learn to build people up; stop tearing them down. Pour on praise and thanks."

"I feel better than I've felt in a long time," Henry said on leaving. "Gives me confidence to have a definite plan to follow."

Later Henry wrote me: "Gridley owes me nothing more but love, to treat me well. He already is paying me what I'm worth to him. I can be worth more to myself and to the public. I need an idea, not more money from Gridley. All good ideas are from God. So you see, I'm learning. For I've got a good idea." His health had improved, too. No more rocks in his stomach.

A month later Henry came to report wonderful happenings: "Gridley was in a bind about his car. Needed a repair job. Garage had let him down. He had to go out of town early Monday morning. Saturday afternoon I told him I'd take it home, repair it. 'Always wanted to get my hands on that car,' I said. 'It is the finest ever made, deserves good mechanical care.'

" 'Yes, yes, indeed,' said Gridley, probably too surprised to say more.

"It was really a work of love for the car," Henry admitted. "That bit about no strings attached bugged me. I repaired, washed, waxed, and polished and got the car back to him Sunday morning. Gridley offered to pay me. I said no, it had been a real pleasure." Henry paused, shame in his face, and said, "Big deal, me washing a car. I kept thinking of Jesus washing the feet of his disciples."

Henry's good news included the fact that Gridley was in Europe, that he had charge of the store and drove Gridley's car daily. Mr. King, who was remodeling an old house, came in for hardware. "You are going to pay top prices for labor," Henry told him, "and your job may not be worth it. I'd be happy to run out to see your property after work and tell you what I think." Henry was still working with Mr. King; "Buy this, not that."

On his next visit Henry brought further good news. Gridley was home with high praise for Henry's work. Mr. King had spoken to his banker and others about Henry. Henry bought a truck and fitted it so that he could do almost any repair job a house needed. He worked only after store hours and bought his materials from Gridley. His business card listed twenty-two jobs he could do well.

By making intelligent responses to the needs of others in his work, Henry was making new friends and liking them. He learned a great secret of life: *we love the people we do good things for.* We love our good work wherever it is done. Love takes time to listen. This Henry had been forced to do. Now he enjoyed it. Love is courteous, honest, kind, and truthful. When his satisfied customers began to tell Henry he was that kind of man, Henry began to value their love and opinion and would not let them down by being anything different.

Henry had also become a part of his community on a volunteer-service basis. He held a workshop at a church to teach boys "practical things they could do at home." He joined a service club. He and his family attended a church and became members. They tithed. He was going on, from wall to wall, and building the other parts of his house of love. He had learned that praise and thanksgiving are both happy children of love. He no longer envied his brother-in-law, but found that he liked the man. Henry learned that God is a good bookkeeper, that the good he did in secret was rewarded openly. Reward always surprised him when it came.

Thinking of his sons' future, Henry wanted to expand, to go on eventually to form a building company. When the money he needed did not materialize Henry came to me saying, "Must be my fault somewhere along the line."

We found the stickler. Because he feared he never could raise as much as he actually needed, Henry had asked for less. "God is not broke," I said. "Your lack of faith is a form of lessening the size of wires, and thus, the power load they can carry. Have faith and *ask for all you need*. Remember, your cause is just; you are working for and with the Spirit of love."

To increase his faith from passive to active, I told Henry to draw a mental picture of his completed project, perfect and performing. To *hear* the sounds of the new shop. To *touch* and *see* every appliance in it. To *smell* the fresh sawdust. Pictures increase faith. Henry was to picture himself working in the shop. And to continue his prayer project. Prayer places our orders with the Soul of the universe. Henry followed through. His faith and work inspired others. Then Henry drew actual plans and made up a cost budget for what he needed and wanted. He was offered more financing than he had requested, and he accepted it realizing that expansion would swiftly follow.

When his shop was completed, Henry's boys worked there every spare moment. He did not give them allowances. He paid them what they actually had earned. He was training them up in the way they should go, building them into men of responsibility and worth. *Work is the teacher.*

Today Henry has a flourishing business and a car like the one Gridley owned. Henry considers it the "finest piece of mechanism ever put together to proudly travel a road and rejoice the heart of man." But he knows that his own body is a mechanism far more wonderful and that by his free will, thoughts, and emotions he can turn his bread to stones, or turn the stones of life to bread.

"If you will take care of the love of others, the love of others will take care of you," I had written in Henry's instruction book. He proved this to be true in his own life.

We are building a house of love and have completed an eastern and a southern wall. But who could live in a house of two walls? Let us now build a western wall.

3   Love: The Healer of Physical Illness

LOVE LIFE

*Decision is the bridge . . . love of life builds a western wall
. . . growing, rejoicing spirit . . . power with an undefeatable
purpose . . . chance or plan . . . years cannot stop you . . .
the light you can't turn off . . . the need for prayer.*

Story from Life: The Man With the Part-time Heart

"Thou shalt love . . . with all thy heart."
Jesus in Matthew 22:37

"IF ONLY I HAD good health—"

Many people apologize for their unwanted situation, actions, failures, and unhappiness in life by prefacing it with that remark. Good health has three sides: physical, mental, and emotional, or body, mind, and soul. Much physical illness has to do with lack of love. For example, let me tell you about Anton, *the man with the part-time heart.*

When Anton came I asked, "What is your problem?"

"My heart is bothering me," he said looking frightened.

"Then let's find out what you are doing that bothers your heart," I said, and took his life story.

Anton was a dark, handsome man, a little overweight, with an air of great seriousness. His mouth was buttoned up tight, his movements deliberate, his speech calculated. At forty-eight Anton was happily married, loved his wife and four children, had no real money problems, liked his work, and owned a fine home, car, and a desert weekend cabin.

Anton's history showed his parents had been poor and God-fearing rather than God-loving. The vague fears of poverty, death, and a God of punishment still bothered Anton. He feared life itself could come to an end—absolute annihilation. He could not sleep without a small light on in the room. His wife never knew why but accepted it.

The crisis that brought him to me was fear of another heart attack. He had suffered a mild one at his office when he was alone one night, and his doctor, at Anton's insistence, had put him in the hospital for a week. His family did not know the cause. They thought he had a virus. The attack came after Anton had heard of the sudden death of a younger friend from a heart attack.

"I am one of the twenty-eight million Americans who already have experienced the first signs of serious heart trouble," Anton intoned solemnly. He continued to quote dire statistics until I stopped him and gave him information from my heart-research file.

"The heart was made to last one hundred years or more," I read. "It pumps blood and life to each of your billions of cells. It pumps your ten pints of blood around repeatedly, moving forty-three hundred gallons a day. It is the sturdiest muscle in your body." I ended with, "Anton, tell me, who and what made it so intelligent? So willing to work? And for what purpose?"

Anton shook his head. "Just nature, I guess."

Anton had no joy in living. Duty, responsibility, comfort, yes. Sex was a little sinful (his early misguided-fear training) and dancing frivolous. Later, when I talked with his wife, I learned she was one who loved to dash into the ocean at night in the nude or to lie naked in the desert sun. Susan loved every breath of life and so did their children.

Anton needed to learn a great deal about life itself, not just his individual share of it. I told him: *"Life is an intelligent power with an undefeatable and indestructible purpose.* The Creative Spirit of the universe never stops short of accomplishment of purpose. Its final purpose seems to be to keep man growing toward the glorious liberty of the sons of God. This surely will take a good many lifetimes. You couldn't die if you tried. Neither life nor death are in the keeping of man. It is God's business and He is attending to it."

Anton wanted to believe. But the stored memories, thoughts, and fears of childhood stood in this way. His parents believed and taught that some were born predestined to go to hell and die. Some would live after death. There was nothing the individual could do about it. Anton was afraid he would not make it.

I told Anton about building a house of love as a means to understand and live within the two great commandments of Jesus. Anton needed to build a western wall, *to love life itself*. And he needed to love with all his heart—full intent and purpose —the entire spirit of livingness.

A western wall, or window, connotes sunset, coming of night, and darkness. During World War I people said of the soldier who died, "He went west." But the great American Horace Greeley said, "Go west, young man," for fame, fortune, and a new chance at greater living. I personally believe that death is a gateway to a new and better life. Anton and I threshed out ideas of what he could and could not accept.

Again I read to Anton from my resource files: "About sixty-five percent of those suffering a heart attack survive. Over eighty-five percent of those who survive go back to work." Anton perked up. I added: "That is because life itself is determined to go ahead. It is the energy of God, a part of God's love. Work with it, and it will work for you. Use it. Go all out. Widen your channel. Let more life flow through you. How can God be happy about you unless you are happy with life itself? You know how you suffer when your children are ill or unhappy. To think that you might die young is discounting the fact that God wins if you live."

I told Anton his fears were denying his wife and children their rightful joy of living. He could not agree. Didn't he work hard, pay the bills? Wasn't he generous? It was slogging effort to get Anton to see that his fears were choking the very mechanism, the heart, through which life flows. He was troubling his heart and his family.

From another source file I read: "Dr. Charles H. Mayo said worry affects the circulation, the heart, the glands, and the whole nervous system. 'I have never known a man who died from overwork,' said Dr. Mayo, 'but many who died from doubt.' " Because Anton respected authority, I read from the dictionary: " 'Life is the vital force whether regarded as physical or spiritual; the presence of which distinguishes organic from inorganic matter.' " I concluded, "You will have to decide for yourself, are you a man, created by God, with a will to live, or a mouse or a mothball?"

Anton's present religious life was not doing much for him. He attended church regularly, but he did not get joy from it. He often came out with feelings of guilt and depression. Yet he was a responsible church member and a consistent tither.

I also read to Anton: " 'It is a great mistake to suppose that God is only, or even chiefly, concerned with religion,' Dr. William Temple, Archbishop of Canterbury, primate of England, once said."

Anton nodded in agreement with the authority of these words, but his fears were still there, filling his heart and my office and tightening his mouth. We went at the idea of fear itself. I gave him the definition I use with my students: "Fear is the painful emotion caused by a sense of impending danger or evil; dread."

"Yes, I do have that feeling," Anton admitted, looking surprised.

We discussed the fact that Anton lived daily with the feeling that something bad, which he did not want to happen but was powerless to prevent, would happen—death. And something good, which he did want and felt powerless to provide for himself, would be denied him—eternal life. "It is enough to kill you," I said. "You will have to cast off that burden and trust life itself and the God who created you. *Decision is the bridge* that leads from one body of thoughts and acts to another. You need a bridge of solid belief and trust. Over this you can walk daily and lead a normal life."

Because he wanted to do the very best for his wife and children, I gave him the following definition of love: *Love is the pure motive of giving greater enjoyment of life to others.* Jesus said, "I am come that they might have life, and that they might have it more abundantly" (John 10:10). Anton needed to let the mysterious power, the awesome force of life, have full play through him. Not to love and use life is to deny God and His purpose for man.

In the mirror test Anton's fears showed up sharply. He was able to see what his family saw. I said, "You are much too well and whole to be acting, thinking, and talking sick ideas. Praise God for the spirit and life and love that are now racing through your body."

Anton had never learned to pray aloud or in the presence of anyone. He stood nervously silent. I worked out a prayer for his daily use: "*Let the Spirit of love work through me and increase my joy in living in every phase of my life. Let my life be a blessing to me, my family, and others.*"

Anton was also to read daily: "Love is the power that makes an intelligent response to the object of its affections. To love life is to respond to it. What we love we become and we keep." Anton was to enjoy using his body, to walk, dance, and swim, to enjoy love-life with his wife and activities with his children, and to feel that the more he used his energy the more additional energy would come to him to be used. He would widen the channel. He had feared that he did not have enough energy, that too much use would endanger his life. But I encouraged him to open up, to let it flow!

His daily affirmation was, "I love life and life loves me/God and life and I agree." I give affirmations to my students as a means of building a memory bank of reality and truth that will set them free from worry and fear. It builds a faith that holds in time of stress.

Anton was afraid to go back to work though his doctor had said he would be all right. I suggested that he go alone for a few days to his desert cabin and take a good look at life in action. He was to take along certain books I would give him, including two on astronomy, and his tripod telescope and field glasses to study the greatness of life of day and night.

Anton was to remember that he would be seeing the same moon that Moses saw when he was taking the Children of Israel out of bondage in Egypt; that Jesus saw when he went alone at night to pray; that the Pilgrim Fathers saw in this new land. He was to think about the *permanence* of life and God's project, man on earth, and to ask which is in charge: chance, life that might stop, or plan, purpose, and power that cannot be defeated. To bring his meditations down to himself and to ask: "Why did God create *me*?" and try to hear the answer. He was to keep busy, not to rest all the time.

"Always a job to be done around the cabin!" Anton said in the manner of a man willing to accept responsibility.

I typed out a directive for Anton to take with him to think through daily: "Your objective is to overcome your fears, either by faith or by argumentation. You have troubled your heart and it had to trouble you. Face the facts behind all this, that you do not want to die ever and are afraid that death ends all. Trust life to take you through now and hereafter. Trust the Mind that created you, that put your billions of cells together, to keep you intact."

So Anton went off to the desert. On the fourth day he phoned to ask if I thought it was a good idea to have Susan go up for a few days. I did. And she went. On her return she reported good changes in Anton. When Anton came home he told me some of the wonders of life working in a seeming desert waste. "Even the tiniest seeds, roots, and plants are determined to live. Thread roots split a rock in search of food. The little animals of many kinds are determined to live." Anton had taken color pictures of some of them. "And the stars. Billions of them! I feel there is life on some of the stars," he said with deep interest.

Anton was obviously improved in health and happiness. He took an earlier-than-usual vacation for a family journey and camping trip. At home Anton was feeling better than in years, but he was still uncertain about life. "At times I feel sure I couldn't die if I tried, but at other times I worry. The difference is that now I'm aware that my emotions do affect my heart action. It lets me know."

"That limits you to the use of a part-time heart," I said. "When you stop worrying about life itself, you will stop bothering your heart, and then it will be a full-time heart and stop bothering you. How well would you function if your boss stood back of your chair all day watching you, afraid that you were going to fail?"

Anton returned to work, but my prayers continued for him to see and accept the truth that life is eternal. Several months went by, then one morning he phoned me, sounding so strange and urgent that I changed my schedule and told him to come on. He arrived inwardly excited, but outwardly reserved as he told me of a "strange experience" the night before.

"It was such a happy, fulfilling time with my wife—you know —well, I was a bit poetic in expressing my joy, gratitude, and all, and I heard myself saying, 'I want us to be together in all of our lifetimes from here on.' I don't know where the words came from. They were spontaneous. I didn't think them up. Then Susan said, 'I think we have been together in many lifetimes.' That floored me. We never had talked about previous lives before. But we talked for hours. We both believe that there might be something to our feeling that we've had former lives together." He wanted my opinion.

I told Anton some of the greatest minds of the ages have believed in reincarnation and that while Jesus is not recorded as having taught it, neither did he speak out against it. Several references indicate that Jesus' disciples believed in reincarnation. It was generally accepted at that time. In Matthew 17:12, Jesus implies that John the Baptist was a reincarnation of Elijah. In Luke 9:18, Jesus asks his disciples, "Whom say the people that I am?" They answered, "John the Baptist; but some say, Elias; and others say, that one of the old prophets is risen again." Most people of the day must have believed in reincarnation. The early Christian Church accepted the idea until the Council of Constantinople, A.D. 553, discarded it by a vote of three to two. Since then the Christian Church has practically lost sight of the idea, but today millions are asking whether we have lived before, and there is a growing literature on the subject. My feeling is that within a few years science will find the truth.

Anton thirsted for further information. I told him that many of the great poets and sages of modern times have believed in reincarnation. Among these were Browning and Tennyson. I typed out for him the following lines from America's great poet, Walt Whitman:

> I do not think that seventy years is the time
> of a man or woman,
> Nor that seventy millions of years is the time
> of a man or woman,
> Nor that years will ever stop the existence
> of me, or anyone else.

The words "existence of me or anyone else" electrified Anton. They do not say how life continues, but that man continues to exist. Anton felt he may have had an experience with a subconscious old soul memory that brought out the spontaneous words he had come to report.

"Why not?" I said as we discussed it. "The very life of man is God-in-man. The Creator who could set up a universe such as we already know, a fraction of what we will learn in even the next few years, would know enough to keep life going once started. There could be no point in stopping it, in wiping out all that nature has gained. Earth is a school where we learn truth. We are on our way to something vastly more important and glorious than we can yet realize. But we can be thankful for it, try to love it, and work with it. *Life cannot die.* If *life* could die, then God would die a little with the death of every man."

Formerly Anton had read only business literature. Now ready to study, he was given lists of books that would help him to expand his consciousness. These included: Du Noüy's *Human Destiny*, Gustaf Stromberg's *Soul of the Universe*, A. Cressy Morrison's *Man Does Not Stand Alone*, Emerson's *Essays*, Jung's *Memories, Dreams, Reflections*, and many others. A little later I added Teilhard de Chardin's *The Phenomenon of Man,* Thomas Sugrue's *There Is a River,* and Arthur Ford's *Nothing So Strange.*

Anton began with Stromberg, a scientist and religionist who was on the research staff of the Mount Wilson Observatory in Pasadena, California. Stromberg taught that a perfect pattern of every organ in the human body is held in "space–time" and that from this perfect pattern, we can, through prayer, repair or rebuild a damaged organ. Anton said thoughtfully, "Then could 'be ye therefore perfect, even as your Father which is in heaven is perfect' also mean a command to your organs, to my heart, for example, to become perfect again? It would help me to believe so."

"Hold to it," I said. "It cannot harm you and may open up a new light for you. Meditate on it, and think of life as the fire that can't be put out."

Anton's prayer program helped him greatly. He changed churches and met new people of high consciousness. "No worms of the dust there," he reported. He and Susan made new friends and were part of inspired and inspiring meetings and "talk-fests."

Not all who come to me for help follow through. Anton was one who did. He built the complete house of love and went on with the program, as we shall in the chapters that follow. There came the day when I said, "Anton, I now take you off of my please-God list and put you onto my thank-you-God list." Anton had accepted as truth that we live after death. His heart troubled him no more.

Many forms of sickness result from not loving life itself. People who find life a burden, who don't enjoy people, and who are so lacking in love of themselves and others that they do not enjoy them are sick most of the time. Psychosomatic medicine today uses facts found in the Bible that have to do with spiritual laws and physical health. In Proverbs we read, "Can a man take fire in his bosom and his clothing not be burned?" A fire in the bosom such as hate, fear, or resentment is an emotional disturbance to the soul. These do "burn" our physical body. I feel that this is often the cause of a stroke. No one can see emotions, but we can plainly see where they have been at work. Some doctors say that about eighty-five percent of their patients are not sick organically, but are simply emotionally ill. Their fears, frustrations, lack of love and laughter, and aimless, unmeaningful living take a toll on their physical health. My vision is that tomorrow science and religion will get together and teach people how to value life and stay well.

Neither money nor the loving services of others can keep us well if we do not love life itself. The one who does love life wants to get well. He benefits by contact with someone who loves him. I have watched this work many times. It seems to me that the sick person is in a negative condition. The healthy person is whole and in a positive condition. The thought, touch, and loving concern of the healthy person communicates inspiration and hope to the patient. It is as if a strong force, like electricity, flows from the positive to the negative, completing the divine circuit of love from helper to patient and back to God. I have seen instant and complete healings with the laying on of hands and prayers by the whole person for the sick patient.

Some illness is the outcome of a desire and need for self-punishment to expiate a real or imaginary sense of guilt. We instinctively want to be in good standing with God. Until we learn to handle life with love and prayer, self-punishment is a built-in attempt to deserve the love of God. Dr. J. G. McKenzie, in his book, Nervous Disorders and Religion says, ". . . an intelligent and well-informed religious experience is still the greatest and quickest resolver of the conflicts which press upon the soul of man in this modern age of ours." I agree and feel that many would benefit if the confessional were returned to Protestant churches. I also feel that healing will come back to the churches. This will follow the widespread conviction that we must love or perish as individuals, a nation, and a world.

Some physical illness is a result of the patient's neurotic need for love. Since he does not love himself, he cannot believe others love him. No matter how much love is poured on, he begs for more and often ends up in a sickbed in his efforts to win that love.

Man's greatest hunger is for love. Young children die without love in spite of perfect food, care, and a germ-free environment. There is much more to this truth about love and life than we yet know.

I have known people who don't want to get well or stay well. When I am asked to pray for health, I ask the student if he is ready and willing to accept the responsibility of being healthy and whole. The first step in good health is to be willing to try to live within the law of love.

To review points discussed so far:

> *Love is the healer:* it leads to work, action.
> *Work is the teacher:* it leads to decisions.
> *Decision is the bridge* over which we cross from one body of thoughts and actions to another.

Throughout our lives we will be faced with decisions. Indecision is a killer. Decision is a tonic. Decisions that lead to greater good give us feelings of needing to express gratitude, thanks, and love. Decisions that lead to wrong actions and further troubles give us feelings of needing to ask for help. These two feelings lead us to the need for prayer.

We now have three walls in our house of love: love of self, love of others, and love of life. But we also need a fourth wall.

4   Love: The Healer of Spiritual Sickness

LOVE GOD

Prayer is the changer . . . be good to your self . . . love works in a circle . . . God has need of man . . . decisions lead to action . . . give it away . . . no place to hide . . . a very big thing . . . more than medicine or money . . . people need people . . . prayer leads to faith.

Story from Life: The Woman Who Lived in a Bottle

> "Thou shalt love the Lord thy God . . .
> with all thy soul."
> *Jesus in Matthew 22:37*

HAPPINESS IS A PACKAGE DEAL made up of many needs rightly met, including self-fulfillment, knowledge of a job well-done, and rejoicing in another's good. But the greatest of these needs is love. We need to give out love, have it accepted, receive, accept, and use love. This completes the divine circuit and releases tremendous powers within us. Without love we are not whole persons nor can we long be happy, healthy, prosperous, or in self-control.

We are building a house of love, part by part, to which happiness will come and make of it a home. Achieving this complete life on earth builds our soul-self and expands our consciousness. Becoming a whole person prepares us for social and cosmic consciousness. We are ready to build the fourth wall, which is *to love God* with our very soul and self. This will add a northern wall to our house. If it sounds too farfetched to say that if we love God, we must make an intelligent response to His needs, then let me tell you about Candy, *the woman who lived in a bottle.*

Candy was an alcoholic. She first came to me at the request of a nurse, Ruth, who had helped to save her life during a "drying out" process at the hospital. Ruth, a former student of mine, had read to Candy from my book, *Change Your Life Through Prayer*, and felt Candy was interested and asked me to see her patient.

That they run from life and hide in the haze of alcohol is proof enough that alcoholics are tragically unhappy. In working with this type of soul sickness, I have found that each case involved a violation of the law of love somewhere along the line. This was true of Candy.

Incapable of taking teaching at first, Candy came once a week simply to talk. We sat in front of the fireplace in my living room, and I listened without criticism, offering love with no strings attached as she drank black coffee, chain-smoked, and relived her life. A nurse and housekeeper lived in her home. She was not allowed to be alone during those weeks. From the first I was able to give Candy the assurance that I cared about her, wanted her to get well and stay well, and believed that she could and would.

Candy was a tall, thin, blonde woman of forty-two. She dressed well. Her surface manners were polite. Her big gray eyes and heart-shaped face still showed some of the beauty she had when she married at nineteen. At my request she brought family pictures of her early childhood and school days, her wedding, her husband and some of his family, her two children, and her mother. The more I learn about a student, the more quickly I can start to help.

An only child, Candy's mother's family had money. Her mother's sister had "married money," and Candy and her mother were quite envious of the wealthy relatives. Her father, however, was a weakling who could not hold a job. Her mother divorced him early and did not remarry. From infancy on, Candy had been spoiled by her mother. When things went wrong, she would fly into a tantrum, and her mother, who needed the child's love but did not know how to train her, gave her a piece of candy "to get her quiet and happy again." In school problems her mother took up for her and unjustly blamed teachers and others. "My

Candy-girl is too sweet to be bad," she would say. The name stuck.

A newborn baby must receive love from others or it will perish. It comes to earth with this need already in working order. The infant cries to demand love and care regardless of the trouble to others. Candy never had come completely out of that infantile stage of demanding love without giving in return. Very early in life, she decided to depend upon the love of others for her happiness and welfare. She worked at her goal in various and devious ways, some deliberate, some unconscious. To excite pity she learned to cry, beg, and demand. If these failed, she turned to tricks.

Thus Candy grew up, considered the most beautiful girl in her town. Through connections with her wealthy Aunt Flora, she "met the right people." One of them was Tom. Candy was so beautiful; could dance, sing, laugh and be so gay; had considerable acting ability; and was so thin and fragile-looking that Tom lost his head over her. She was a tender flower that needed to be protected, taken care of all her life, he said. These were war years, and driven by emotions of threat to life, love, and future happiness, Tom and Candy were married hurriedly.

Their first child, Timmy, was born while Tom was away at war. Candy kept contact and visited Tom at his various posts. The second child, Elizabeth, was born before Tom was out of the service. When Tom came home, Candy and the children moved out of her mother's home into a house with Tom. But he was soon disenchanted by Candy's utter selfishness, lack of responsibility, studied deceit, inability to train the children, and temper tantrums, though between times she could be sweet, lovable, and charming. She had a way with people. They loved her in spite of her shortcomings, Tom told me.

Tom got a divorce, gave Candy a substantial and carefully protected settlement, and later married a "practical, sensible girl." They had no children. When Timmy and Elizabeth reached the age of decision, both chose to live with their father, which the court allowed. Timmy, now twenty-two and away at school, and Elizabeth, a college student at home with her father and stepmother, had not seen Candy in several years.

The crisis that induced Candy to work with me was her fear that "her family was closing in on her" to have her committed as mentally incompetent. "They say to keep me safe so I can't drink, ruin my health, and waste my money. But it is really because they hate me," she said, her mouth pouting in a four-year-old way. "Tom's wife knows I hate her for stealing him. He forced me into a divorce to marry her. She was twenty-four. I was thirty-six. Tom's wife is a social climber. She was a nobody, worked in the office. She wants a big wedding for Elizabeth when the time comes. They don't want me there. They have influenced my children to hate me and desert me. I, who gave them life!"

When I can find the fears that torment my students, I can start to work with them toward solving their problems. Because it is true that "perfect love casts out fear," their fears show what part of love is missing in their lives. Candy had both open and hidden fears.

Candy's present fear was of loss of freedom, of "being locked up and managed." She had frightened her family terribly. On a long, lone drinking spree at home, she had gone into an unconscious stupor. Her cleaning woman, who had a key, on a hunch went by on her way home from another job, saw the curtains drawn, felt uneasy, and went in. She phoned for help, and Candy was gotten to the hospital in time.

This fact I used later to help Candy realize that there is a Spirit of love in the world, that no one ever is alone. "God must still have need of you; He found a way to pull you through," I said. Candy soon changed my words to her own as we worked together: "God must still have need of me, or I would not be."

Candy's hidden fear was that she had lost forever her power to charm. Her age of infancy was over so far as others were concerned. She had found that being a bottle-baby (an alcoholic) led to degradation and death. There was no place to hide from the truth—change or die. I had to lead her to see that point for herself. She felt utterly alone, having quarreled bitterly with both her mother and Aunt Flora. Deep loneliness is a soul problem.

Candy's greatest unconscious fear, which she understood and agreed with when I explained it to her, was of what would happen to her after death, when she had to account for her lifetime on earth. This is, of course, a fear of being rejected by God, a fear that there is no unmerited and unlimited love, but some kind of punishment instead.

She trusted me, wanted to move into our home, and felt hurt when I refused. This was in the years before my husband died. One morning we woke up to find Candy's car in our driveway and a sober Candy, huddled in blankets in our patio. She had run away from home rather than meet with Tom's attorney.

I talked with the family and Tom. They were willing to drop proceedings against Candy provided she work with me, which she wanted to do. She lived on in her home and came once a week for teaching. I put aside a book I was working on and devoted a great deal of time to her. She needed every second of it. She would show up without an appointment and would phone me often during the day, or even at midnight. She needed to talk it out, to receive constant reassurance and praise at every point of progress. From an instinct deeper than reason, Candy knew she had to have love or perish.

The following are some of the facts Candy had to accept before she could get well and hope to stay well:

1. *Her drinking was suicide in slow motion.* She was saying, in effect, "I don't amount to anything and I ought to destroy my-self."

2. I explained to her that, though nearly always unconscious of the fact, we attempt to punish ourselves for doing anything we consider to have been evil, sinful, and wrong. This is natural and necessary until we learn the better way, because we want to wipe out our transgressions against God and be at one with Him. If God turns from us, we are lost indeed. I made it clear to Candy that I do not believe God punishes us, ever. Rather, we consciously and unconsciously punish ourselves. I also told her about

the law of sowing and reaping, cause and effect. This is inexorable. The law of compensation and balance is just one proof of God's love. Candy's healing depended upon her feeling worthy of life. Her drinking was actually a search for God.

3. Candy would have to work with a purpose—love of God—and build that northern wall. Since she could not yet love herself, she had to start with the idea of loving God, the source and nature of goodness in the universe. Having had very little religious training, Candy's idea of God was simply that "there must be something or somebody who runs things." But she was frightened at the idea of loving God. "I don't even know him," she protested.

"You love love itself," I said. "All your life you've wanted to get others to love you and to do good things for you with no strings attached. That's all *you* have to do—*good things for others with no strings attached*. That is one way to love God, to work for other people. We help the Spirit of love get good things done."

Candy needed to learn that doing good things for others is not pouring it on in the way her mother had with her. *Good for another* always gives him some degree of freedom. Candy began to see that her mother had helped to put her into a prison of ideas, emotions, and reactions to life without having meant to do so.

4. Candy's sense of guilt was so deep it stood in the way of her recovery. So I told her that she still had her original goodness with which she had come to earth; that conscience never dies, sleeps, or can't be drugged, killed, or thrown away. Nothing can stop it from working. This is a truth about life and all people. We have free will and so have conscience, know right from wrong, even when we try to hide the fact from others and ourselves. But never can we hide from God, the standard of love and good, and we know that. This is a matter of truth, recorded in space–time and cannot be erased.

I worked out the following for Candy's use:

Definition of love: *God in action*. This action builds courage and self-reliance in individuals. It does not cater to weakness or selfishness. If it is love, it leads to work and to more freedom in some form for someone.

Definition of God: The Power that created the universe, all people, and me for a good purpose.

Her daily prayer: Let the Spirit of love work through me and change me to all I ought to be.

Her daily affirmation: *There is nothing bigger than God.* This she was to use every time a fear, worry, problem, or decision to be made arose.

My students are sometimes required to write out what they believe and to tell me how those convictions are working and why. One of Candy's examples was this: "It seems ridiculous that I can do anything for God, but I can. God has a purpose for man. He needs people to develop and to grow until they are as intelligent and as good as Jesus Christ was. When I am good and live by love, I am making an intelligent response to God's needs. This is a very big thing."

Candy knew little about the Bible. I told her the simple stories which reveal great truths about God, man, and their relationship. Always I stressed the fact that *love is the healer of every unwanted condition known to man.* That the Spirit of love can build up a good habit and dissolve a bad one. For love is the power that cares enough to do enough.

Slowly at first, Candy began to build the southern wall of love for others without realizing she was doing so, at the same time building self-love, the eastern wall. She stayed evenings with a sick woman whose tired daughter needed rest. In cooperation with the nurse, Ruth, I found much work for Candy to do. Her first year with me was given almost entirely to learning, establishing truths, voluntarily serving others, and improving herself generally. I encouraged her to take instruction to learn to read to others. This she did and learned to read dramatically and beautifully. Finally, Candy did volunteer work in a hospital for mental patients and in rest homes, where the old, the unhappy, the neglected, the bored, the lonely, and the unoccupied need love more than medicine or money.

People do need people. Candy discovered for herself that God does have need of man to help carry out His work on earth. She learned that love, being a form of energy, works in a circle. You can't give it away without it coming back to you multiplied. Wherever she served, everyone loved Candy, for Candy loved love itself. She received more attention and appreciation than ever before in her life. It was given freely. She didn't have to beg for it or to "do tricks." Candy blossomed under it.

We often talked of her strong northern wall. "If we love God and feel that we are working for Him," I said, "No cold wind of adversity can chill us; no cold rain of unwanted and unexpected circumstances can get through to us. No pain, no threat, not even death itself can worry us for long. We have eternal life and we become conscious of it. To think of working for God is to think of our final freedom as a greater being, whatever it is God has planned for man."

Candy grew stronger in body, mind, and spirit as she served others. She found new joy in living through work. The whine left her voice. Some of her former beauty returned. One of the men patients at a hospital recovered and started to call on her. Candy began to entertain the hope that maybe. . . .

But life was not through with Candy, and Candy was not through with her housing project. As it turned out, she was going to need that strong northern wall. In fact, she was going to have a use for every stick and stone of all four of her walls. "All I have learned, . . ." she said without fear or self-pity.

"All you have become," I added, "which is much more than you realize."

Candy hadn't taken a drink since she first came to me. She did not take one when the storm broke. For six straight years the storm beat down upon Candy's house of love. First, she lived through the heartbreak of not being at her daughter's wedding, of being totally ignored. Next, of not seeing her son graduate with honors. Then her mother became ill, helpless, with no one but Candy to take care of her.

"Looks like God still has need of me," Candy said, "or I would not be assigned to that job and be able to carry it through." This she did, until her mother died. Candy had just gotten established again when her Aunt Flora was taken ill with no one but Candy to help. She said Candy was so cheerful and gay, "like when she was a girl," that she felt better when Candy walked into the room. Of course, for *love is the healer!* Candy served faithfully until Aunt Flora died.

But Candy had not seen either of her children in years. When she was alone, again "picking up the pieces," she met a good man, an ex-alcoholic, and they married. They lived happily and quietly, learning more and more of truth. Together they helped others. "We feed the sheep," Candy once said to me in her bright way, recalling the words of Jesus to Peter in John 21. She often called me to say, "We are giving another sheep party."

One day Candy's daughter came to see her voluntarily. She had problems. Could Candy help her? "Looks like God still has need of me," Candy told me. And her work with her daughter also brought the son back into her life. When Candy first came to me, she could not bear to take the mirror test. But finally she could stand before the mirror and recite the whole of the 139th Psalm, which says in part:

> Whither shall I go from thy Spirit?
> Or whither shall I flee from thy presence?
> If I ascend up into heaven, thou art there:
> If I make my bed in Sheol, behold, thou art there.
> If I take the wings of the morning,
> And dwell in the uttermost parts of the sea;
> Even there shall thy hand lead me,
> And thy right hand shall hold me.

There are twenty-four verses in this Psalm. Verse 18 contains the line, "When I awake, I am still with thee," which so inspired Harriet Beecher Stowe that she wrote her immortal poem, "Still, Still With Thee." Set to Felix Mendelssohn's music, it has become part of the soul and consciousness of thousands. This Psalm is especially inspiring, helpful, and comforting to the one who is trying to break out of a prison of bad, destructive habits. Candy reduced it to the firm conviction, there is no place where God is not!

Prayer is the changer of lives and affairs. Prayer is talking things over with God and your own soul-self. Prayer expands the consciousness and opens the mind to hear God's perpetual calling "Come up higher!" Through prayers that led to faith and work, Candy changed her life for the better and worked through to a happiness she had not known before.

All prayers embodied in truth and love are answered. In her darkest hour, when Candy realized she would die if help did not come, she tried to pray and then lost consciousness. But let us notice that her cleaning woman "obeyed an impulse" and went to Candy's home and got her into a hospital. And Ruth was assigned as her nurse. The Psalmist is right about it. The love, wisdom, will, and power of God are ever present. But *we must ask for help* if we want help.

We now have four walls for our house of love. But so far they are just standing in air. We need to put a solid foundation under them. Since we are working with spiritual ideas and laws, not bound by wood and stone, we will find a way to go ahead with our project.

5 Love: The Healer of the Sick Mind

LOVE INHERENT GOODNESS

*Faith is the pattern-maker . . . wings are for lifting . . .
build your house on a rock . . . voice of conscience . . . no
matter what . . . gods, devils, and duds . . . man is not
alone . . . the record speaks for itself . . . express or explode
. . . faith in good leads to harmony of life.*

Story from Life: The Man Who Needed Wings

"Thou shalt love the Lord thy God . . .
with all thy mind."

Jesus in Matthew 22:37

WE ARE LEARNING some of the parts of love because we must love
or perish. Unhappiness is a danger signal. It is a warning that
something is wrong in our life. We should learn what it is and
correct it, because unhappiness can lead to sickness and death.
By discussing the points of love as parts of a house, we are building a house of love in which happiness will dwell. This means we
are building our individual soul-self and expanding our consciousness. We have learned to love ourselves, others, life, and
God. These are the four walls. The fifth need is to love inherent
goodness, which is a part of the nature of God and is alive everywhere. Inherent means the love is there whether we see it or can
believe it or not.

To love that goodness inherent in God, ourselves, others, and
life itself is to work for it and with it. It is to promote and uphold
this goodness, everywhere present, which in turn puts a foundation under each of the four walls of our house of love. Unless our
walls are anchored securely to a strong foundation, the storms of
life can and may tear our house apart. Jesus tells us to build our

house on a rock. Rock means faith. Our faith must be in the goodness in the World Soul, and so in all that God created, including ourselves. No one ever can separate himself from that love, but he can be blind to it and ignore it. The life experiences of others can help us to learn. So let me tell you about Don, *the man who needed wings.*

Don was a tall, thin man of fifty-six years, happy enough with his wife, two married children and his work as a creative designer, but so terribly unhappy with himself that he was sick. Pale and hollow-eyed, he could not sleep without sleeping pills, took tranquilizers on the job, and suffered from chest pains and indigestion. I asked what his fears were. He said, "A little more of things," bringing his hands together in a squeezing motion, "and the men in white will cart me away. My doctor says I am cracking up mentally and should see a psychiatrist. Won't do it. No faith in them."

After further probing, I felt Don would be harmed rather than helped by the mirror test. His distress was so deep he could not bear to study himself. Every case of mental and emotional problems I have ever worked with had to do with not enough love or a violation of love. Not a single one of these anxiety-ridden, fear-filled and worried persons had ever been radiantly happy. This was true of Don.

Don had left the "God of his fathers" in college days. His father's brother was a preacher. "That altar call, people crying and frightened by hellfire—emotionalism for children—give your heart to Jesus—made me sick and often I could not eat Sunday dinner. Uncle Bud was an actor and a salesman. He won if he frightened people, and it helped him to raise money. I came to despise the man."

Well-grounded in his Bible by word and letter, Don had missed the spirit of it. The tragic result was that he had given up religion entirely. The pressures of modern life such as atomic war, communism, economic problems, crime, and immorality, had become personal threats to Don. He felt "all boxed in." He had no inner protection against those outside pressures as they came closer and closer upon him. He questioned the existence of God and the possibility of eternal life. I feel that to doubt the existence of God is to be, in some degree, mentally ill. To think of God as punishing man, to fear an actual living hellfire, is, I think, an indication of a soul sickness which might well be classified as mental illness. Don was "sick of himself."

Don's mother had sent him a copy of my book *Change Your Life Through Faith and Work*, but Don never had attended a New Thought church; did not know that I often lecture and teach in them. In fact, he knew nothing of the powerful and rapidly expanding New Thought movement of which I am a member. Don was "through with churches." To help Don see that he had not lost all faith, I said, "I am a religious practitioner. I teach the spiritual laws and how to solve your problems by learning to live within these laws. And I am a lifelong Methodist. Why did you come to me?"

"For one thing, you have helped others. And because once . . ."

It took Don awhile to word it. One Sunday afternoon, when he was ten years old, he went for a walk alone in the woods near his small hometown in the Midwest. "It was spring. Wild flowers in bloom. Everything green and pretty. I picked some blue violets for my mother. The creek, with the sycamore tree leaning over it, made everything seem quiet, peaceful, unhurried. I thought heaven must be like this. But I was afraid I was a lost soul. Hadn't joined the church. Hadn't given my heart to Jesus. I felt guilty. I sat down in the grass, in the warm sunshine, and bawled. After awhile I felt calm, peaceful, good. I felt that nothing in the world ever would hurt me. That Uncle Bud was wrong. I was happier than I ever had been. But it didn't last. I want to recapture that feeling. What did it mean? Was I a little off, even then?"

"I think you were very much on," I said. "I think you had a genuine religious experience and did some original thinking. It was good." I told Don of some of the experiences of the great mystics and seers. William Blake saw angels and as a child saw St. John and had other so-called supernatural experiences. Today some researchers are saying that such happenings are natural, that some people have evolved further than others. Extrasensory experience is now common to many.

"That day in the woods I felt there was someone near me. Someone who loved me. As a kid, I believed in angels as I believed in Santa Claus. But it's all gone. I'm hollow. I've lost something," he said sadly.

"What do you want me to pray for?" I asked.

Don managed a small grin and said, "Wings. You know what happens when you try to swat a fly—it just raises its wings and leaves you feeling foolish. I need wings to rise and fly away from it all," he said, waving his hand in a gesture of out and up, indicating that something else would have to help him, that he could not help himself. The possession of wings implies power to direct our flight. Don actually wanted to direct his own life and affairs rather than run away from life.

"Freedom," I said. "Every soul wants more and more freedom. It is our destiny. Symbolically, you are right. Wings are for lifting. You need wings made of love and faith. Your mind will direct the flight. It is a matter of learning that prayer is asking, love is desiring, and faith is believing. Where are you going when you fly away? Suppose you had enough money to retire right now. What would you do with your freedom, with your life from here on?"

"Study," Don promptly replied. "Try to learn something I could believe in fully and that would give me the feeling of peace I had that day in the woods."

Don long had wanted "something to believe in fully," but he had not done anything about it! He had stood aloof, sulked, and blamed others, the church, and the world for conditions that made him fearful and unhappy. When I confronted him with the facts, he gave me defensive arguments; everyone was wrong but himself. When I asked him questions about some of the latest findings of science relative to religion and the nature of man, life, and God, Don had no answers. He was astonished at my questions. He had stopped learning. In religious thought and feeling,

Don was still in the days and emotions of his childhood. These were no match for today's world.

To Don's tirade against world and church, I said, "Your opinion in any matter is worth only the sum of your accurate information. You need new accurate information if you are to get well and stay well. The truth you need and are hungering for does exist. But you will have to be willing to seek, ask, knock, and find it. Then, to live it. Life does have meaning. But each person must find it for himself."

Don had descended into a valley of doubt. "Life itself did not force you into that valley," I said. "All of us on our journey of life on planet earth come to valleys of doubt and fear, where we wonder about the established teachings and our abilities. It is a part of soul and consciousness growth. Our need is to keep right on walking, trying to climb the other side of the hill that makes the valley and to find the level, higher, and safer ground on the other side. You did not cross the valley when you found yourself in it. Maybe the hill on the other side looked too steep. So you made camp and stayed there."

I told Don some of the wonderful things happening in modern churches that are walking hand in hand with modern science, about building a house of love, and that he needed to start with a foundation of rock-bottom faith. Don understood well what it meant to build his house on a rock after our discussion. My written instructions for him included facts and directives. Some of the points were:

Faith is a deep belief in the inherent goodness in oneself, others, life, and God; and that this goodness will eventually win over every obstacle and threat to the happiness and success of the human race. Don was to learn how to put down one section of his foundation at a time, as he built a general background of faith. His daily prayer was: "Let the Spirit of love work through me, heal my body, mind and affairs, lift me up, and give me wisdom and peace." His daily affirmation was, "God loves me, no matter what!"

Everyone has feelings of guilt. No one does the right thing all the time. Every infraction of the law of love, real or imagined, lessens our faith in ourselves, and to a degree, in others, in life, and in God. This is why Jesus said to love God with our mind, our very thoughts. Jesus knew the truth about our sins, or mistakes. Sin comes from the Greek word that means "missing the mark" and has to do with the game of archery. Everyone misses the mark. But God continues to love us anyhow, just as we are, right where we are.

Don became really interested, and I carried him further into the truth. Jesus told the sick man, who doubtless felt guilty and unworthy, "Thy sins are forgiven thee." The sick man accepted the fact and doubtless felt worthy to be healed. This so greatly increased his faith that he was cured (Matthew 9:1–8). The answer to prayer depends upon faith, Jesus said. All the teachings and works of Jesus proved that faith depends upon love. The sick man was healed when he felt God loved him and so he could love himself.

Finally, Don saw that he could build wings of love and faith that would lift him out of that valley of doubt, despair, and set his feet upon a new and higher ground of conviction. He took the following steps out and up:

1. He learned that love leads to action. Repeated right action leads to success. Faith leads to trying for greater goals, but always the right goal is one that will give us, in some degree, more freedom from, or to. Simplified, Don could increase his faith by increasing his love and putting it to work.

2. Don had to love himself, his own inherent goodness. Working with pencil, paper, his memories, and my questions, we found much good in Don's life. He was a faithful husband to his wife, had taken good care of his children, and had made quite a sacrifice to send his son through a university. He was a good employee and valued the life, liberty, and property of others. He was honest, truthful, and far more upright than he had come to believe.

3. Don needed a worthy pattern to follow in order to build his own self-esteem and self-image. I told him there was no better

pattern to follow than Jesus, the Christ-consciousness Man. I helped to give Don a new concept of the Great Teacher, who said that others could learn to do the works he had done. This was an entirely new concept to Don. It is one of the main points of the New Thought movement.

4. In trying to increase his faith in others, I led Don to reconsider the church. It has come from the inherent goodness of millions of individuals who loved, worked, and sacrificed for it from its beginning to this day. The very university Don's son had attended was a church-related school; indeed, many of the oldest universities in Europe and America were started by churches. Our American Constitution and freedom for the individual are rooted in the Judeo-Christian faith and the church. "We can sit here today in safety and peace, learning together, because other people who loved enough to do enough have died for our right and privilege to do so," I reminded Don.

From the church, we went on to other points: schools, law, and the many organizations for human good, protection, and learning which represent love at work. When Don began to remind me of instances of inherent goodness in others, I felt we could go on to the next point: inherent goodness in life itself.

We traced some of the story of man on earth as science now knows it. We saw the way life works, that it never stops and never is defeated, but tries new ways if old ones close. Life is always growing out and up for more and more happiness and livingness for the individual man. We talked about the wonderful human body and how it can heal itself, and about the miracle of the birth of a child. We discussed the march of civilization. Don finally said, "Yes, life knows what it is doing. Life itself is good."

5. We talked of God. Don needed to outgrow his childhood conception of a God of vengeance, a tyrant, and take a good look at the God of modern science and the space age, a God of love and wisdom beyond our present ability to understand. "You must put your mind to this," I said. "You must make this knowledge, love, and faith your own, not just words from me. You will have to build new tracks in your brain."

My typed work for Don included passages from books that would be helpful to him in building his wings and exercising them. Included was this passage from scientist A. Cressy Morrison's book, *Man Does Not Stand Alone*: "Science recognizes and gives full credit to man's craving for higher things, but it does not take seriously the dogmas of the hundred jarring creeds, though it does see in them all paths which converge toward God. What science sees, and what all thinking men know, is the unbelievable value of the universal faith in a Supreme Being."

What this belief Morrison talks about has produced through the ages, we call civilization. Don began to see for himself that he had been suffering from a bad conscience. His sins were of omission rather than commission. He felt guilty for having wasted years of opportunity to learn which could have led to greater knowing and doing and happiness. He had simply stayed in that valley of doubt until it had brought his soul to despair.

6. Don agreed to "really work at it." I agreed to provide him with carefully selected reading materials in the four fields: the record of the inherent goodness in ordinary human beings, in life, in God, and in the man Jesus. Don was to go to church. To pray and stay away does not increase faith, and does not show love. We owe moral conduct, financial support, love, and attendance to our churches. The ministers and church organizations are there when we need to be christened, comforted, taught, married, or buried. If we don't like the church of our childhood and want one big enough for the space and electronic age, we have the right to start a new one.

7. Don was so hung up on the evils and turmoil of our day that he needed new truth to set his mind free. As a defense against fear, he had been storing up hate. He needed to love with his whole mind, to care greatly, and to think about the good that is going on. I gave him material showing some of the good that great organizations are doing to create a better world for all people.

It is true that we have gods, devils, and duds in every age. They represent different stages of soul growth. By their actions they show others how they are using their free will, whether for good or evil, and how much love and faith they have or lack. But they all have goodness inherent in them. All were born to be free, and eventually will break out of their own and other man-made prisons. Tyrants, rebels, and dictators are temporary. The soul of man is permanent. Tend to the growth of your own soul. God will take care of what is His business. He knows what goes on.

8. About prayer and loving with his mind, I told Don that according to science we have ten billion cells in our brain which we can use for thinking. Each cell is a servant. When Jesus said to love the Lord God with all your mind, he must have known that there is a way to do it. We talked about the value of prayer and meditation. Meditation is meeting with the harmony of the Spirit and prepares the mind to go before God with our prayer. Prayer is the changer.

As time went on Don overcame the hurts of his childhood, was faithful in his daily work, and began to stabilize. But he was not yet ready for work. I suggested that he take a further leave of absence and go back to visit his boyhood home. So he and his wife drove back to see his parents; his father was then eighty-seven and his mother was eighty-five. He had not seen them in years. I received cards from Don and his wife saying, "Nothing is as big as we remembered it." And, "The creek is still there, the violets still bloom." Don's prize story about his visit was the attitude of his parents. They told Don he was too old-fashioned in his religious beliefs. They were members of the New Thought movement.

Don, who had been so "sick of himself," came to respect and love himself because he was a child of God trying to learn and grow. He built his house of love, carrying through on all the points we have covered so far and those we are yet to study. Moreover, Don finally "gave his heart to Jesus" as the greatest teacher for human happiness the world has yet seen. He became so emotional in telling me that he was embarrassed. "Emotion is a good thing," I said. "I believe in religious fervor; it widens the heart, opens the mind to God, and definitely helps the soul to grow. Trust your religious feelings. Use them. Express or explode. Don't be afraid to turn yourself on, to let the joy of life flow through you."

Points for the expansion of the soul-self and conscious awareness of good:

1. Forgiveness is a basic need for mental and spiritual healing. Don's concern about world evil was saying in effect, "They threaten my safety and I hate them for it." Hate is a defense against fear. Don's fear and hatred were forms of asking, "Why does God permit them to do this, if there is a God and if he loves me?" Don learned to forgive all—himself as well as others—and to view the "human situation" with new understanding. He learned that evil puts itself down. All evil finally will fall of its own weight. Even war someday will be wiped out of the mind of man forever. Life no longer threatened Don in his new high area of consciousness.

2. Don thought he was "losing his mind," but he found it sound and greatly expanded when he studied the healing power of love. Love is a living energy which like fire, turns other things to its nature. In the immediate future love will be used as the healer of many conditions that have led to mental illness.

For the most part mental health has been measured in negative terms. Freud worked with sick people and described their behavior as the norm of human nature. Some worked with rats and other animals and described their reactions to given situations as true of all human beings. Today, the big swing is toward defining mental health in positive terms, and healthy people as the normal ones. The brilliant work of Abraham Maslow has been compiled in a paperback book titled *The Third Force* by Frank Goble in "a revolutionary new view of man." This work restores man to the dignity of being a child of God and not merely an animal. Love is the keynote of this new psychology of man. The ability to respect and love others and to respect and love one's self is the sign of the mature and well-integrated person. In an article in *Mental Hygiene*, Dr. Benjamin Mehlman of Kent State

University said, "If man is the measure of the universe, then love is the measure of man and the hope of mankind."

3. In his book, *Human Destiny*, Lecompte du Noüy says that: "Independently of any rite, of any church, there has always existed in the world a religious spirit, a desire to believe, a desire to adore without restriction, a desire to humiliate oneself in total veneration, a desire to elevate oneself by approaching a conceivable but inaccessible ideal. It is this desire which is of divine origin, because it is universal and identical in all men. Religions, doctrines, dogmas, many and varied, often intolerant, are on the contrary the product of men and bear their mark."

The above helped Don to "find his original feelings of religion" and proved to be wings to his spirit.

In our housing project, we now have four stout walls anchored to a strong rock foundation that will be stormworthy in any problem of life. We have learned to love self, others, life, God, and goodness inherent in the Soul of the universe. But we also need floors in our house of love, smooth floors to walk over from situation to situation in life.

6 Love: The Healer of Guilt Feelings

LOVE THE HARMONY OF LIFE

*Harmony is the joy-bringer . . . love is being in tune with
God . . . walk to music . . . put floors in your house . . .
come to order . . . put a song in your heart . . . sexual
freedom is not free . . . love is the cement that holds
families together . . . search for the law.*

Story from Life: The Young Woman Who Was Out of Tune

"On these two commandments . . ."
Jesus in Matthew 22:40

IN ORDER TO BUILD our soul-self and expand our consciousness we
are building a house of love where happiness will dwell. We
have completed five of our points: love of self, others, life, God,
and inherent goodness. Now we need to love the harmony of life
that obedience to the law of love gives. This will put a floor in
our house.

In the two great commandments Jesus gave the formula for a
fulfilled life for the individual, a happy marriage, a great society,
and a better world. Obeyed, these commandments are the only
method of coexistence ever presented to the mind of man that
allows the individual to be his highest, happiest self, while allow-
ing all other individuals to do the same, with harm to none and
good for all. Obedience to the law of love binds the human
race together in a common purpose of joy and greatness in
living.

No two people can live a married life together and hope to be
happy without obedience to the law of love. Love is the cement
that holds marriages and families together. But it takes a lot of

doing to convince some of the troubled young couples who come to me for help. For example, let me tell you about Karen, *the young woman who was out of tune.*

One cold, rainy day when I was alone, the bell rang and I opened the door to a slender young woman with unkempt hair, wearing a soiled blue suit and battered shoes. A stranger to me, she had come without contacting me. She had beautiful black hair and eyes and milk-white skin; but her rough, demanding manner spoiled her good looks.

"I'm in bad trouble. I want you to help me out," she greeted me, using her whole body to convey her message.

Seated, but not relaxed, in front of the fireplace, the girl told me her story as I questioned her. Karen's parents were divorced before she was of school age. Her mother married again. Karen said she "hated" her stepfather, her half brother, and her half sister. She felt schoolteachers had been unfair. She had wanted to become a great singer. When she lost out in a finals contest, the teacher told her she had a good voice but needed "more stability." Karen "just hated her for that."

Some church people who heard Karen sing in a school program had paid for her private voice lessons. But when she lost the contest, she "lost heart, started to date Ted," and became pregnant by him. "The church people turned on me, and the woman said I ought to be ashamed as long as I live. She said I'd never live down the disgrace nor would my child after me. I never tried to sing again."

Karen and Ted married when she was seventeen. When the baby was six months old, Ted left her and she got a divorce. Next she met and "fell madly in love with Dean." Another pregnancy and marriage followed. Dean left her when the baby, another girl, was a year old and divorce followed.

As Karen poured out her story her mouth twisted in hatred; her eyes flashed with outraged feelings and a desire for revenge. She said that she received child support from each of the two fathers and welfare for herself and the children. Her crisis was that she had spent all of her welfare check for a new record player and albums of recordings. "I've got to do something all day," she defended her act, "and music keeps me from going nuts."

Karen had seen my picture in the newspaper announcing a lecture I was to give. "I felt you, being a good churchwoman, would help me," she said. "I need money bad. I have no money now for milk and food for the kids until the next welfare check comes."

The girl showed such good possibilities and sensitiveness to life that I felt I had to make that meeting count. We went to my student mirrors and I said, "Show me how you would walk out on the stage to sing to a great audience."

Karen's face and eyes took on new life. "Like this," she said excitedly, acting the part.

"Very good," I complimented. "How would you do your hair?"

Karen's slender hand flashed into her big soiled red handbag and came out with a comb. She twisted and arranged her hair until it looked attractive and I told her so. "And what kind of dress would you wear?"

Gazing into the mirror, lost in the drama she was living, Karen said, "Bright yellow. Goes good with my hair and eyes. Long, touching the floor, and I'd put a yellow band in my hair, like this, and ..."

"As you stood there, waiting for the orchestra to start up, would you want the audience to admire you or to pity you?"

"Admire me, of course," Karen answered, puzzled.

"I can tell you a lot about how to get people to admire you," I said, and we went into my office.

Starting with the most basic ideas of the power of love and attraction, I led Karen to take an honest look at herself and her marriages. We reviewed the quarrels, and why each husband had deserted her. She confessed she could not keep house, nor cook, nor sew; could not manage money; and had run both husbands into debt.

"What did you give them in return for their love and support of you?" I asked.

"Why, I got in bed with them," Karen said simply, surprised that I should ask. "And I did not go out with any other boy while I was married to them. I was true." But she felt uncomfortable when she told me. Our conscience always is judging us on the inside, no matter how we behave on the outside.

Finally I asked, "Are you bringing up your two little daughters to be failures in life, to ask for pity, or are you training them to be a success, to win admiration and love?"

Karen began to weep. "I've had a rough path to walk on all my life. Everybody tricks me. I thought you, being a church-woman, would give me money. But you're only giving me talk!" She twisted her hands together and glared at me angrily.

Anger denotes fear and a desire to have things changed quickly, before something unwanted happens. "I tithe my money far ahead," I said, "but I can drop other work and give you a tithe of my time to help you get your life straightened out. Jesus did not go around giving people money. He taught them how to make a success of life. That is what you need to know, for otherwise you will keep right on making mistakes that lead to problems and unhappiness."

"All I need is just some money right now," Karen insisted, drying her eyes. It was an ultimatum.

"Well, then," I said, "I will call your caseworker and get it straightened out. Or the store, and have them take the things back, or put them on a charge account and give you the difference in cash."

Karen sprang up and spat words at me: "I thought you'd be kind and help me, but you're just mean like everyone else!" She dashed from the room and out of the house, slammed the door, and ran to her car. I made no effort to stop her.

The thought of Karen's two children possibly facing hunger ruined my dinner and my night's sleep. The next morning I went downtown, bought a length of yellow ribbon, got some money from the bank, and drove over to Karen's house about noon. Karen, in a soiled blue robe and dirty cloth slippers, her hair stringing around her face, answered the door.

"Brought you a little gift," I said, holding out the package, and edged into the room without being asked.

"Might as well come in," Karen said sullenly, trying to hide her sense of shame. "I guess you know the truth anyhow."

It turned out that Karen actually had bought the record player and albums four days before she saw my picture in the paper, and had settled it all with her welfare worker before she called on me. She was not in need of food or money, she admitted.

"Your acting ability shouldn't go to waste," I told her. "There is a way to make it pay. You should learn about it."

Karen stood still and looked at me with childlike wonder. "Aren't you going to cuss me out?" she asked.

"No, I'm going to love you and help you, if you'll let me," I replied, and put my arms around her. There is little point in telling people God loves them unless there is someone to put his arms around them. When we speak of love, it helps to show it.

Karen was surprised and touched by my interest in her and accepted my offer to help. I told her she needed to get in tune with life itself, to establish order in her home. "You should keep your house, yourself, and the children neat and clean, because it will make you feel happier," I said.

"Nobody sees me," Karen argued, on the defensive.

"You see you. You're not a nobody. You're very much of a somebody. The way you see yourself builds a picture in your mind, a pattern you will unconsciously live up to. Always look your best for yourself and your children."

"The kids are too young to know or care," Karen insisted.

I told Karen that Dr. Ray Lyman Wilbur, when president of Stanford University, said that even the pieces of furniture in the home have an influence for good or bad on the children's lives and development. I explained further how ideas and pictures drop into the subconscious mind, from where they dictate part of our lives or even most of them, if we are not careful.

"Is that why I hated that old ragged brown sofa in our home?" Karen asked, interested.

"If it was ugly, out of tune with beauty, you doubtless did not like it. You were born for beauty and harmony. When we love beauty and harmony enough, we try to create them." And that is how our studies together began. Karen set a date that afternoon to come for training.

Karen learned the points of love as I have explained them here. She needed to build a floor in her house of love. "You need something to walk over from room to room, which means you need an orderly way of life, not a hectic, frantic one. Something solid to stand on and to believe in as a guide when you have decisions to make." Karen was quick to catch the picture of her new self, her new home.

I told Karen to walk to music all through life, to take the two love commandments and make a song of them in her heart. We talked a good deal about the necessity of being in tune with life itself. "Think of people on earth as playing and singing in a great song festival that God is conducting; remember that you are an important part of it; if you do not perform your part well, the whole project will suffer."

Karen, looking big-eyed, exclaimed, "Oh, I don't want to be a sour note!"

Her daily prayer was: "Let the Spirit of love work through me and help me to order my life and affairs into a harmonious whole and become a part of the music God is playing."

Karen enjoyed the mirror test. I had only to tell her the desired role and she would begin to create it. She acted out being a good mother, speaking to the children and training them, conducting herself toward other people, and expressing her feelings about herself. Soon she started to teach the children to act out "being good and using manners." I told her that her children would learn and retain more through the method of praise than they would through scolding and punishing. But I added that she must discipline the children and always explain to them, "We do it this way because. . . ."

"It sure works out," Karen began as she told me about her new way of living in a house of harmony. "If I blow my top and scream at the kids, I'm not making an intelligent response to their needs. I have to be in tune myself so God can sing through me. The greatest violinst in the world cannot play a concert on a violin out of tune," she said, repeating her learning, always very certain that I would continue to love her, would not stop trying to help her, as long as she tried.

Soon Karen was enjoying order in her home. "It is prettier," she admitted, "when the kids' sleeping clothes are not on the floor." I encouraged her to love beauty and told her that fitting the parts to the whole was adding music to the great harmony of all life. *Love is being in tune with God*, and we all ought to stay in tune with our higher, singing selves. Karen enjoyed the jingles I gave her as lessons, and she often sang them, using the tune of a current popular song. One was: "I'm singing a song of love and laughter, and only good can follow after."

Karen's definition for love was the one I had given Henry, the man who turned his bread to stones. She memorized and quoted it to me often: Love is what you feel that makes you do things for certain people for free that you wouldn't do for anyone else for money. When Karen proudly brought me a perfect apple pie she had baked for me, I knew she understood the meaning of love.

We had a good many talks about morals and manners. She began to contrast her ideas and ideals with those of some of her girl friends, and to want to meet new friends. From the first, I had set as a goal for Karen to fit herself for a paying job and thus go off welfare. Welfare was making her feel she was an inferior, a minus person, and added to her guilt feelings. I encouraged her to become a plus person, and that it would help her to sing her best. In time, she got a job selling recordings in a music store. She gathered quite a following of young people who bought records from her. I visited her home at regular intervals and praised her for her improvements in her house, child care, and her own appearance. She had begun to read with a purpose, to cook, sew, and manage money.

Then one day Karen said, "I would like a boyfriend, but I'm

afraid of what would happen. I'm clean now and rid of the guilt feelings, because I'm serving my kids in love and behaving, and God loves me. I want to stay that way. So what do I do about this boyfriend need?"

We were in my office and had been watching a cat climbing the bay leaf tree just outside the window, heading for the mockingbird's nest. "You have free will," I told her. "Without it, you'd have to mate, hate, fight, run for your life, kill or be killed. You'd be like that cat, a slave to your instinctive desires. But you are not like the lower animals. You have grown to freewill choice. No one could have forced you to come here today. You *decided* to come because you *believed* it could better your life. You even went to considerable trouble to arrange things so you could come here. Always choose the good, the honorable, the moral thing to do, even if it means self-denial or hard work at the time. Choose the way of self-respect, self-love, and self-confidence or be left with new problems."

After further talks on the subject, when I felt that Karen was adult enough to marry again, I suggested she set that goal, and not just to seek a boyfriend. She agreed. We set up a prayer program for it. I suggested that Karen invite Dean for a Sunday dinner soon.

"Only if you will be there too," Karen said quickly, "not alone with *him!*" Her reaction confirmed my feeling that they still cared for each other. Karen talked about him a good deal but had not seen him in some time.

So I went to Sunday dinner and met Dean, a likable young man suffering from a deep inferiority complex and a load of guilt feelings. He showed genuine affection for his little daughter. The look of surprise and approval on his face when he saw Karen's "new home" was good to behold. His words were not surprising. "Why didn't you do things like this while we were married?" he asked, noticing the new yellow kitchen curtains Karen had made and the very clean rooms.

Karen introduced me as her teacher. Dean wanted to know if

Karen was taking voice lessons again. "I always thought you ought to and hoped you would," he said. The bond of music was a strong one between them.

"Oh," Karen explained, "Mrs. Mann is not that kind of teacher. She's teaching me how to be a better person; how to live happily ever after."

"Are you going to marry again?" Dean asked hastily, cutting another generous slice of roast beef for himself, and adding, "I didn't know you could cook. We used to live out of cans and TV dinners. My God, how I hated that stuff! Do you have a boy-friend?"

Karen sent me an eye appeal for help.

"I've decided Karen ought to marry again and stay home, keep house, cook, and bring the children up right so they will eventually make a good marriage and stay married. Yes, I am going to help her get a husband worthy of her and the children. She has now become good marriage material." As I spoke, Dean put down his fork to listen.

The children behaved very well, a fact not lost on Dean. I outstayed Dean, saying that Karen and I had more lessons to do. He left reluctantly, and accepting Karen's offer, he took a large section of her delicious chocolate cake with him.

A few days later, Karen phoned me, greatly disturbed. Dean had come there unannounced the night before "with ideas," she said. "But I just told him no, that I am not a cat climbing a tree, or a bird fighting for my life," mixing her points of free will and the prison of instinctual desire. But Dean got the message. He approved of her stand. He went away but the following day he phoned me, wanting to know, "What did you mean about Karen being good marriage material?" And what had I done to make her "so attractive and everything and so grown-up?"

"Marriage is for adults only," I told Dean. "Being twenty-four does not make an adult of you. There's much more to it than years."

Dean was willing to learn. When he came for his first appointment, I felt he would make it eventually because of some things he said. "About sex. A man has to degrade himself, pay for it, and walk away, or he has to marry the girl if he gets her into trouble. It's not easy to be a man these days," he informed me unhappily.

"It never has been easy to be a man," I told him. "But a real man knows that using his free will to control his instinctive sexual desires is what separates a man from an animal. The animal cannot say no. The man can. There is only one right way to handle the sex urge, and that is inside of a happy marriage. Sex itself is not a cure-all. But love at work is. Sex without love is degrading to both the man and the woman."

"I guess you are right," Dean agreed. "But marriage these days costs money."

"There is no such thing as sexual freedom," I said. "Sex is a privilege and it has a price. Irresponsible sex sets up a series of costly results and an ever-widening circle of problems to both sex partners and to the society in which they live. We have the proof in the high rate of venereal disease, sterility, death, abortion, and child parents—many of them only thirteen or fourteen years of age—plus the suffering and expense of a generation of nameless children who will give plenty of trouble tomorrow. If you want your heart broken, go take a look at the little girls waiting for their babies to be born. Go visit a juvenile hall. Sex is not free, any way you look at it. Marriage or nothing."

"It is true that I want my little daughter brought up decent," Dean said thoughtfully. "And I am unhappy about the mess I made of marriage. It has held me back in my business life. It is a mark of failure against me. And of course it hurt my parents too."

I talked to Dean about the rising costs in taxes that are hourly increasing to take care of people who cannot or will not take care of themselves. "Your generation will have to help to build a better world through better people, or pay for it all your lives," I said. Finally, I told Dean that a good wife is a business and social asset. She is not an expense, but an income for the husband who knows how to win and hold a good, mature woman's love. "It takes two to sing the song and do the dance of life, and the two must agree to make a marriage work," I reminded him.

Dean and Karen came to me together for counseling until they married again. They continued to learn and to build and live in a house of love.

Points to remember:

1. The floor in your house of love is made up of your desire and attempt to live within the two great commandments of love. Harmony of life and living under love ties all of your earthly activities together.

2. *Harmony is the joy-bringer.* Joy is the stimulator which leads to self-expression. Self-expression needs to be under the law of love. Expression of the self in wild riotous acts against the rights and comfort of others might give the offender joy, but it is out of order with the Soul of the universe. Only right order leads to love. And love is never out of order.

3. We need to express our love in song, laughter, fun, doing, and being. Make your life a song of love and your love a song of life.

4. *Love is the healer:* Love leads to work.

5. *Work is the teacher:* Work forces decisions.

6. *Decision is the bridge:* Decisions lead to the need for prayer.

7. *Prayer is the changer:* Prayer leads to faith.

8. *Faith is the pattern-maker:* We receive what we believe. Faith leads to the harmony of living.

9. *Harmony is the joy-bringer:* Happiness and joy lead to a search for a law that we can always depend upon to hold our happiness.

But who could keep happiness in a house of four walls, on a sound foundation, with floors, but no doors? We have more building to do.

7 Love: The Healer of Youthful Rebellion

LOVE THE LAW OF LOVE

*Law is the protector . . . spiritual laws execute themselves . . .
spare the rod and spoil the child . . . lawbreakers are
unhappy . . . Build stout doors in your house . . . keeper
at the door . . . living is for learning . . . knowledge of law
leads to courage.*

Story from Life: The Hippie Who Was Never Happy

"On these two commandments hang all the law . . . ."
Jesus in Matthew 22:40

OUR OBJECTIVE in this study is to become whole, fully mature
persons. All else being equal, we will mature fully in our physical
selves. But the mental-spiritual self is always in the making. The
biblical promises made to man for the advancement of his soul,
for health, wealth, and happiness are made under law. In the
two great commandments Jesus gives man the highest of the
laws, the law of love, and says that all the other laws hang on
these two commandments and are dependent upon the law of
love for their fulfillment.

To love the law of love is to try to live within it, to uphold,
teach, and honor it. Some modern parents do not understand the
spiritual laws and so they "spare the rod and spoil the child." A
rod can be an instrument for punishment or a measuring stick of
what is right and what is wrong in human conduct. If the laws
are taught to the growing child, he learns how to become a
responsible and a happy person. If the teaching is neglected, he
becomes a breaker of the spiritual laws and the laws of man and
a most unhappy person. An example of this is Chuck, *the hippie
who was never happy.*

Chuck's mother, Mrs. Lovell, came to me saying, "We have tried everything else and nothing has worked with our Chuckie, so we want to try religion. When he was ten years old a neighbor boy of sixteen committed suicide. No one ever knew why, except that he was always unhappy. I think we have been frightened about Chuckie ever since. We've given him everything he wanted. But he is never happy for long."

The crisis that brought Mrs. Lovell was that Chuck, twenty-two and a school dropout, had lately met a girl who worked in television. She had "nagged and shamed Chuckie into getting a job." Chuck had stolen a hundred and fifty dollars from his employer's cash till to "buy a handsome dress for his girl friend who needed a special one in her work." Chuck, following an old pattern, was sure his parents would pay the man. But the employer had Chuck put in jail. The parents bailed him out immediately and offered to pay the man, but he refused to accept their money. "That young man needs a lesson," he said.

Chuck was an only child. The Lovells were in business for themselves. From birth, the boy had been cared for by house-keepers. The parents sometimes left at four in the morning, returning late at night. Mrs. Lovell's recital showed that both parents had piled gifts on the boy in expiation of their sense of guilt for neglecting him. They had lost love and respect for each other and battled for the boy's love.

One of Chuck's childhood practices was to take money from his mother's purse or from the current housekeeper, and buy candy or other gifts for the neighborhood children. "We finally had to lock up the money and give Chuckie a daily allowance."

The parents failed to see that Chuck was making a bid for love. He had learned from them that if you want someone to love you, you give him a gift. Irresponsible and dependent upon his parents, he cleverly pitted one against the other. With the assurance of Mrs. Lovell that Chuck did not use drugs in any form, though he strongly upheld the right of others to use them, I asked her what she wanted me to pray for. "Why," she said, seeming surprised, "for this horrible charge to be dismissed; for that man to accept our money and forget the whole thing." "That would be adding to the boy's delinquency," I said. Mrs. Lovell was angry and resentful. But I knew I could work with Chuck only if both parents cooperated. Chuck's father had washed his hands of the matter and had gone to bed sick, to get out of it. So Mrs. Lovell and I came to an agreement.

Chuck came to see me wrapped in an attitude of defiance. He was an attractive boy with keen gray eyes, clean, well-groomed, and appropriately dressed in expensive hippie style. His dark hair reached his shoulders, and he carried a pair of king-size dark glasses. He lounged into my office in a sullen and belligerent manner, which was a defense mechanism. I liked him. After a few attempts to get him to talk, I said: "You might as well let them lock you up. It's obvious you're not going any place anyhow. You have no work to do, no goal to reach, no battles to win, no truth to find out, no mountains to climb, no points to prove and no pride to defend. You don't even have liberty to defend. You are just a vegetable. You might as well be put into the soup kettle and really go to pot."

After a moment of angry silence, Chuck exploded with, "That's not funny!"

"No, it is tragic," I said seriously, "because it is the truth. Your parents spoiled you. Clipped your wings. But you let them. You hate them because you fear for your own future, with good cause. You are afraid you'll never make it, so you fake it. You need to learn how to haul your own freight."

From the first, Chuck enjoyed mental tussles with me, which gave me a clue to his potentials. He was a child of promise. He tried to put me on and argued every point.

"Your man Jesus also wore long hair," he jibed.

"Not in defiance. He didn't care much about outside appearances. He cared greatly about the inside of a person. He knew enough about spiritual laws to turn the world over. He had something to say, to do, and to teach that would help all

men though he knew they'd crucify him for it. He was a Man."
"He was a rebel. A nonconformist. So am I." Chuck shot the
words at me, trying to look superior.

"Cool it, haul it, and bury it," I countered. "You're a hide-
bound conformist to hippie ideas and half-baked thoughts of
people who depend upon others for their bread. You don't talk,
you only mouth clichés, slogans, and hippie jargon."

"Your generation is a failure. You believe in war. My generation believes in peace and love," Chuck defended.

"No you don't. Unless you first love yourself, have self-respect
and self-confidence, you can't love others. It is psychologically
impossible. Your parents catered to your every whim and
whimper to hold your love because they are not happy. They
have not yet found the way of life that works. But you appear to
be smart enough to want to learn. Your parents robbed you of
your God-given right to suffer for the results of your mistakes
and wrong acts. By paying the cost you would have learned to
be a responsible person. Until you are a responsible person, you
can't love yourself, or anyone else. Without love, you generate
hate. Hate generates war."

"Your generation failed and robbed us of a future," Chuck
sneered.

"In points we failed, because we are human beings. But my
generation gave you the automobile, airplane, radio, television,
computer, improved health care and schools, plus time to enjoy
the good things of life. We have kept everything open for the
individual who wants to make good on his own. It is easy to
point out what the other fellow is doing wrong, but painful to
look at one's own faults. Responsible people do so and find it
pays off."

Next Chuck tried to defend the flower children, a hippie group
in San Francisco at that time.

"They are trying to pin a gardenia on a garbage can and call it
a flower garden," I said. "So long as their physical bodies are
dirty, their minds vacant, and their morals and spirits disordered,
there is nothing beautiful in their life-style. Cleanliness is next to

godliness. Order is heaven's first law. Beauty results from the parts being fitted in likeness to the whole. The flower children are living contrary to nature and common sense."

My replies were not entirely lost on Chuck. Yet he could not give me a definition for love, beauty or happiness. He tried to defend the rights of the drug culture under the Constitution.

"They are in prisons of doubt, fear, and indecision. They have not met the challenge of life, of being responsible persons. It is responsible people who have to pick up the pieces, pay the bills, and save their lives in hospitals."

That day and for some time later, Chuck hated the word responsibility, but in time it became a rod and a staff to him. That day I said, "Responsibility is the dividing line between self-approval and self-hatred. So take your own measure and see where you stand."

When Chuck had run out of slogans and was ready to listen, I asked, "Chuck, what are you good for, if anything?" It was an honest and earnest question born of my real desire to help him, and Chuck was quick to recognize the sincerity of it.

"Well," he said hesitantly, "I can drive a car real good. Never smashed one up. Never had a citation for a moving vehicle accident; never had a parking ticket."

"That's wonderful," I complimented with honest enthusiasm and praise. "If all youth drove that well we wouldn't have such high automobile insurance rates, and careful youths like you wouldn't be paying for the careless ones. How do you account for your good driving record?"

"I read the laws. I can tell you every change made last year in the California Motor Vehicle Code. I know the law and I obey it." There was firmness in his voice and pride in his eyes.

We then talked about the need for obeying laws. I told Chuck that man-made laws have a purpose: protection of the individual's life, liberty, privacy, and property. God's laws have a purpose: a perfected man, for in no other way can a man with free will ever become really free or remain free. Acts outside of love lead to prisons of some kind for the offender. Love proves the existence of law, and law proves the existence of love. Outside of love there is no safety, happiness, or freedom for the individual and the world.

Chuck had only a little religious training. Some of his parents' housekeepers had been churchgoing women who exposed him to some training. He understood the two great commandments only enough to quote them. In a very simplified form I told him the story behind them.

"People of that day who did not want to live the kind of life Jesus advocated, who did not believe that any individual had the powers he ascribed to all men in potential, felt he was dangerous. If that man won, they reasoned, a lot of vested authority would be out of business. So they tried to find reasons for having him put to death. One group had failed to trap him into making self-incriminating statements. On the occasion when he gave the commandments, another group was laying a trap. A lawyer, 'tempting him,' asked, 'Master, which is the great commandment in the law?' The answer the Master Teacher gave has influenced the world ever since and is the base on which our American Constitution, freedom, and rights for the individual rest. It is what got you out of jail on bail. Before Jesus, there were some twenty-three hundred rules of right action which the people were supposed to live up to, some on pain of death. Jesus said all of those rules could be reduced to one—the law of love—and it has only two parts: love God and love people, starting with yourself."

Then I picked up my old red-letter King James Version Bible, which had been my mother's, opened it to Matthew, chapter twenty-two, and asked Chuck to read the story aloud. As he read, his voice took on strength. He began to enter into the spirit of it. Something opened in his mind. At the level where all minds touch in the Mind of God, Chuck understood my desire to help him and trusted me. Our work began that day.

Chuck liked the housing project I recommended, and he saw quickly that his house of love needed doors equipped with strong locks. I typed out the following for him:

1. Doors in your house mean the conscious use of your free will.

2. Your conscience is your doorkeeper. It tells you what is good and what is bad, what to accept and what to refuse. Your conscience is like the compass in your car, which always points north and tells in which direction you are headed. You can refuse to obey it, drive south when you ought to go north, but you'll know the difference and have to admit it by a use of your free will. Your free will can override your conscience and get you into trouble.

3. With your free will you say, "I want to" or "I don't want to." Your conscience as your doorkeeper says, "You *ought* to" or "you *ought not* to." The test for which is right is the lock on your door. *That lock is love of the law of love.* It is there to protect what you value.

4. Your locks will also protect all you have become through soul growth, as well as keep out all that would destroy you. Strong locks mean that you will have to *accept the outcome* of your free-will choices, decisions, and acts. You foot the bill. To do this is to become a responsible person.

5. To make your free will and your conscience work as a unit takes practice. You feel a desire you want gratified. Your free will, according to past habits, will suggest various ways of doing this. Your conscience will say no, you ought not, to some desires and yes to others, according to the law of love. You will have to pay for it. Is it worth the time, energy, money, and soul growth it will cost you?

From these points of understanding, his need, and the law of love, Chuck moved right along with the plan we agreed upon. He was to sell some of his play pretties and his electric guitar, which he had never touched, to collect money to pay the man from whom he had stolen. He was to get a job so he could be ready to pay the attorney also.

I kept at Chuck, who first pleaded that his parents would pay, until he realized that accepting that way out was dodging responsibility and losing freedom. Every instance of breaking the law of love harms us to some degree. Chuck finally agreed he would have to meet the bills himself, and began to think of other things to sell to raise money. "Most of them I didn't want and never have used."

Chuck's mother was outraged at his selling the things. "He will not get ten cents on the dollar of what we paid for them," she complained to me. Chuck held out and proudly showed me his savings bankbook with the first deposit. I told him he had taken steps toward a future freedom; that only responsible men could long remain free.

Chuck got a chauffeur's license and a job driving a light delivery truck for a business house. But his sense of responsibility, knowing when to open and close the door of freewill decisions, had to be developed. One day he took time out for a long lunch with a hippie friend and some merchandise was stolen from his truck. Chuck rushed to ask me what to do.

"I didn't lock the door of the truck, and I guess I didn't lock the door of my house. I guess I ought to pay for that stuff, be responsible for it," he decided. "It will cost me a whole week's salary. I'll have nothing left," Chuck worried.

"You'll have character left, and a sense of pride that will help you to keep on being a responsible person," I said.

"Yeah," Chuck miseried, "I shouldn't have gone with Creedy when he asked me. I should have said no, I got a job to do. But I didn't."

"Doors have hinges," I reminded him. "The choice was yours, open or close. But not all is lost. You've learned that wrong decisions lead to what you don't want and don't want to have to pay for."

"Was I ever stupid!" Chuck groaned.

"Living is for learning. Make your mistakes pay you dividends. Tell your employer at once, say you want to pay for that merchandise, and ask to keep your job."

Chuck phoned me that the employer had agreed and was much pleased with Chuck's attitude. "Now I got three big bills to pay off. Next time, I'll lock my doors!"

"Every time," I injected, "when you don't want to lose something of value."

Working with Chuck was never easy. Once he showed up two hours late for his appointment with no excuse, and I refused to see him. "You didn't catch it, you kicked it," I told him. "Your share of my lifetime for today has been thrown away. It never can come back. If you show up tomorrow at nine we will go on with the program."

"And I thought you preached love!" Chuck sulked.

"I do. I am proving it. I care too much about your highest good and eventual freedom to add to your present delinquency." I closed the door. Chuck was five minutes early the next morning.

Surprisingly, Chuck tried to be faithful in his daily prayers: *Let the Spirit of love work through me, strengthen my will and conscience, and help me to accept my responsibilities.*

Chuck's hippie friends, bored with idleness, never left him alone for long. At one point Chuck was so eager to get away from his parents' quarrels and their overshadowing of his attempts to grow up, and the necessity of constantly having to refuse his friends and stay on the job, that he packed to run away. But he felt enough responsibility to come and tell me.

"Are you out of your gourd?" I scolded. "Stay, finish the court case, and be grateful to your parents that they are giving you free room and board while you learn how to earn. Come all the way out of childhood into maturity and manhood before you take off. Living alone is for responsible adults only. Make new friends. Get into a new area of consciousness with successful and happy working people." All of which Chuck did.

Chuck had a good mind and many fine qualities. We talked about his inheritance: his parents were good people, but they had not known how to train him to become a happy and responsible person. I asked Chuck to look into the possibility of going back to school to study law. Through prayer, pestering, love, honest praise, teaching, and strict discipline on my part, and

Chuck's awakening to the fact that there simply is no place to hide, he kept on the job.

Before his day in court came, Chuck repaid the money to the man from whom he had stolen it, and had a long man-to-man talk with him about his trying to become a responsible person. Every right-thinking adult wants to help searching youth. The case was dismissed. Chuck paid the attorney also. His parents were so pleased they offered to send Chuck on a trip to Europe. But he refused it and started summer school instead. Then I did not hear from him for some time, beyond an occasional telephone call.

When he came to see me again he was grown-up and stabilized, a young man headed toward a career in law going East to school. He wanted to take the mirror test again. As he stood there with the air of a responsible young man, and the look of a conquering crusader, I asked, "Well, what do you see now?"

"A great lawyer," he said a little self-consciously, quickly adding, "in the making." He adjusted his tie and stood a little taller. "Some day I'll marry and live in a house of love." His jaw tightened; he looked at himself critically and his eyes confirmed his strong words: "And my kids will be brought up to accept responsibility. If they buy it, they'll pay for it!"

Back in my office we talked further. "There are hundreds of needs for law," I said, "and more coming up all the time as population and human relation pressures increase. If you will build a consciousness of what is really right and really wrong for yourself and mankind, you'll be a great lawyer. Remember that in nearly two thousand years no one has ever stated it better: *On these two commandments hang all the law.* Some day, the law of love will be the law of the land. Keep it in mind and work toward it." Chuck had learned to love the law of love. I knew he was safe and needed no further help from me.

Points to remember about loving the law of love:

1. *Love is the protector* of me and mine, you and yours, and stands between us, protecting us from each other. Spiritual laws are self-executing and are God's guarantee of justice for the indi-

vidual, both accused and accuser. Eventually our laws of the land will follow the laws of God because our desire for justice and our respect for the individual are forms of love—the nature of God at work.

2. *The laws of God flow down from the principle of love.* A principle cannot be broken. Laws can be ignored and broken. Law is the defender, the protector, the governor of man.

3. *Desire for justice* leads to a search for truth. What is good? What is bad? What frees man? What imprisons man?

4. *Laws of the land* lead to both conviction and freedom, punishment and reward. To know that justice is to be had for all men under the law of the land leads a nation to God.

5. *Knowing that under the spiritual laws* justice is to be had for all men by a power higher than man leads to the conviction that God is love and man is forever safe. This conviction gives the individual the courage to do greater things than he has done before.

We have learned how to live within the first seven points of the law of love which we need to build our individual house of love. But we still have no windows in our house.

8 Love: The Healer of the Fears and Boredom of Old Age

LOVE THE CREATIVE POWER OF LOVE

Courage is the lifter . . . false prophets . . . fear leads to problems . . . love is a fountain of youth . . . time is measured by events . . . keep your windows clean . . . you will take it with you . . . courage leads to trust.

Story from Life: The Couple Who Stopped Their Clock

"On these two commandments hang all . . . the prophets."

Jesus in Matthew 22:40

WE ARE BUILDING a house of love in which we shall find complete fulfillment in life, becoming whole, mature, integrated, and happy persons. We have covered so far seven points of the law of love as given and implied in the two great commandments. Point eight is this: *we must love the protective, progressive, creative power of love.* We need to love this creative power that is in love and witness to its promises and accomplishments in our lives and in the lives of others. To do this is to put windows in our house of love. This is necessary at any time of life but especially to older people, as shown in the case of the Wilsons, *the couple who stopped their clock.*

Wesley Wilson, seventy-four, and his wife Ruth, sixty-seven, came to me for prayers. Their crisis was a fear that they would not be able to pass the automobile driving test which was coming up soon for each of them. Thus they would be helpless, stuck without a car even to go to a doctor or to church. They drove to my home from another county in their six-year-old car, which was clean, shiny, and in good order, with evidence of past loving care. The Wilsons told me their story.

Some six months before, they had sold their home up north and come to live in southern California for the climate and to be near their son and his family. Two months later the son was unexpectedly transferred out of the state. The Wilsons missed him, his wife, and their five grandchildren. Lifelong Methodists, they attended church but had not made new friends. Ruth used to play the piano in Sunday school at home, but in their small apartment they had no piano. They said now they watched television and listened to radio "all the time." Bright, normally happy people, the Wilsons had had a long and very happy life together and could not account for their feeling of "what's the use" and a mounting sense of fear.

"What do you watch and listen to on television and radio?" I asked.

Mr. Wilson sighed and told me about the news and other programs that disturbed them so, concluding with, "We just don't know what the world is coming to." Mrs. Wilson nodded in unhappy agreement. Then they tried to outdo each other in reporting the bad, threatening, fearful things in the world, America, their town, their neighborhood, even the apartment house where they lived.

They had bought books which reported the "frightful conditions, terrifying to read, much more to think of as coming to pass." They had sent money as they could to various organizations said to be working against all those evils, and they felt guilty that they could not send more because the total picture seemed one of utter hopelessness. They felt trapped and afraid.

I listened carefully until they had run down, and started to repeat. Then I said: "Do you suppose God is really dead as reported?"

They were too shocked to answer. A Methodist—thinking God is dead!

"Or," I continued," is it just that God is not big enough to handle all these problems? Which one of them is bigger than God's creative power, wisdom, and love?"

After a moment of their silence I continued, "There is nothing wrong with you two good people," and our work began. Being a lifelong Methodist myself, we understood each other. Methodists feed you first and ask about the state of your soul after that. We went into my kitchen and made coffee. Talking all the while, we carried it and the freshly baked lemon pie I had made for their coming out to the patio. We talked on, for Methodists are great talkers, and enjoyed the warm fall sun, the green citrus trees, the blue jays and doves, the flowers, and the peace of God over the beautiful fall day. I provided them with a large shopping bag to gather lemons, oranges, Rangpur limes, and guavas from my trees, and a clear plastic bag for flowers, while I went back into the house and typed out some material, the essence of our talk-out. By points, these were some of my directives to them:

1. Stop listening to false prophets

Prophets of doom always have been with us and today some of them make quite a profit out of prophesying dire events to come. If they can frighten people, they can get them to listen, send in money, and support their organizations. Some of these prophets are honest but have lost their faith in God, if they ever had any. Never believe in a prophet who does not believe in a God of love, law, order, and power.

Prophets of doom have no real solution for the evil situation. Money will not provide soul growth, and nothing less than the soul growth of millions can solve our problems.

2. Nothing evil is bigger than the love and wisdom of God

The God of the Christian religion and of modern science is a God of progressive good. A God big enough to create and maintain the universe as we know it even now knows what to do when nations and thieves fall out and when growth requires change. Everything a prophet says must square with the love, wisdom, and power of God, or it is not true.

3. Dictators always fail

The average rule of a dictator is fourteen years. The pendulum always swings back to sanity, love, and a higher level of consciousness of the greatness of God and of man. God and His love and man and his free will are forever. Love is the greatest power in the world. It creates only good. It is creating good even now. We all need to learn more about the great good that love is accomplishing for human beings in the world today and for a better tomorrow. Today there are more people working for abundant life, truth, beauty, safety, freedom, happiness, understanding, comfort, and sheer joy of living than at any time in human history.

4. Example of a good prophet

I say that no man has ever yet been half devout enough,
None has ever yet adored or worship'd half enough,
None has begun to think how divine he himself is, and how
    certain the future is.

I say that the real and permanent grandeur of these States
    must be their religion,
Otherwise there is no real and permanent grandeur.

So sang Walt Whitman, our great American poet. He is recognized as one of the spiritual giants who saw good everywhere. He saw it coming for our day. And it is here.

5. Time is measured by events

Many older people forget that the purpose of life on earth is soul growth. With former duties suspended, they start to die unless they start to do greater things than before. If we let our energies pile up, unused in ways which we desire and can approve, if we don't have enough interesting and meaningful things to do, we become bored and unhappy. We stop trying to do new things. Next we become convinced that we can't do new things. *The result is we stop our clock.* This is what you are suffering from now: in effect you have stopped your clock. Time is measured by events. Love is action and action is an event.

Wind your clock and get it going! You do this by becoming happily involved with people, principles, and ideas you wish to promote. Love goes places; it sets out to accomplish definite results. If it is love, it goes to work, always.

6. Take your problems one at a time

You have been looking at a total problem: unevolved man. We are happy when we accomplish things, but unhappy if we are faced with too many problems which we don't know how to solve. If they are not handled, we become fearful, which in turn creates new problems. Concentrate on a few points and get them done. You personally cannot stop riots, campus burnings, the ten thousand sins around us. Don't worry that you can't. Concentrate on the one or two things you can do and do them well.

7. The older we grow the more love we must show

Start by loving yourself. Accept yourself just as you are. Love your wrinkles and don't dread or resent growing old. Some people avoid older people. There are two reasons for this: First, surveys show that many old people are definitely opinionated, set in their ways, selfish. The other reason is that some people are so unhappy themselves that they dread growing old. They hate to be around older people because they are reminded that death, for which they are not ready because they feel they have not yet lived, will come. Because of their own unhappiness, they show dislike for older people.

But the beautiful, unselfish, learning souls grow happier with the body years. Today, this class of older people is holding the good of the world together and inspiring youth. Age has far more love to give than youth. And more patience. Age has a greater understanding of the necessity of morals for the survival of a nation. Follow through on your program of love-outs and witnessing as we have discussed it. Love is a fountain of youth; keep it flowing.

8. *Your daily prayer*

Let the Spirit of love work through us and give us interesting, fulfilling, and happy things to do hour after hour and day after day the rest of our lives. Let our good health and happiness be an inspiration to others.

Remember that all prayers are really asking for more of life, a sense of happiness, more secure and better livingness. Your prayer will enlarge your heart interests, and let more of God's love flow through you to others. Through this prayer you are asking to be unlimited in consciousness and places to serve. Old age is a good time to learn new tricks.

The Wilsons came in with their bags filled with fruits and flowers to take home. After they had read my typewritten directives, I got out my cardboard and paper materials and told them how to build a house of love, explaining the points as we went. When we came to the foundation, Mr. Wilson sat bolt upright and said, "Ruth, that's where we've been amiss—we lost faith in the inherent goodness of God and man and ourselves, I'm afraid." His eyes twinkled with good humor as he added, "Would you say it was dry rot in the foundation or chewing away of termites? Those prophets-of-doom termites!" We all laughed heartily and felt better.

Ruth, her warm brown eyes expressing approval of her husband's wit and wisdom, nodded in agreement.

We went on with our project, put down floors of beauty, order, and harmony, talked of walking to music (all Methodists are expected to sing and heartily), went on with building stout doors of free will, and acknowledged our connection with God-Mind through our individual consciences. Then I said, "We have now come to the part of our house of love which you two good people need right now: *a love of the creative power of love itself.* To understand and work with this power inherent in love is to put windows in your house—large windows—in every one of those four walls.

The Wilsons were to remind themselves constantly that God's love is sufficient for every need of man. The intent, purpose, and plan of God is sufficient for man's future, no matter how foolish or criminal, selfish or greedy some of the individuals of the human race still may be.

To get their clock running again, the Wilsons were to go into action with the love-out program as a witness to the power of love which we had discussed. Mr. Wilson, who was a vigorous and stimulating talker when he liked his subject, was to gather not less than four items, examples of the power of love at work, from old or current news items, concerning each of those windows: eastern, love of self; southern, love of others; western, love of life; and northern, love of God. He was to use these sixteen points of truth—good news—as evidence that things were growing better in spite of appearances to the contrary.

We went to the mirrors and acted out their neighborhood love-out program. Then we turned to a time of worship. Ruth played the piano. We sang Charles Wesley's beautiful hymn, "Love Divine, All Loves Excelling," and reminded ourselves of the love of God and the promise of eternal life and daily help on earth. After a moving and convincing prayer by Mr. Wilson, they set out happily for home.

Methodists got their name by being methodical. I felt the Wilsons would carry through. Later, by their phone calls and visits, I learned what they had done.

They had gone out one afternoon a few days after our conference, when children were coming home from school, to call on some of their neighbors. They had baked a big batch of cookies cut in animals and other shapes and made colorful with sugars, fruits, and icings. They had divided the cookies by dozens and put them in clear plastic bags. At the first door a little girl answered the bell and said, "No! We don't want to buy anything, not even from old people, Mommie said."

"Here," said Mr. Wilson, holding out a bag of cookies. "We are giving them away. We're not selling anything. We are neighbors up there," and he gave their names and address.

"I used to bake a lot for our grandchildren," Mrs. Wilson quickly chimed in, "but they moved away. I baked so many it would be a shame to let them go to waste. Do you like cookies?"

At that point a harried mother, with a baby in her arms, came to the door to see what was going on and listened to what the Wilsons said.

"Well, for Christ's sake," said the woman, "I didn't know there was anyone left who gave away something good for nothing, unless it was to sell more of the stuff."

"We aren't selling anything," Mr. Wilson spoke up. "Love does good with no strings attached. We're offering love."

The woman stood looking skeptical. The little girl continued to show an animated interest in the cookies so colorful in the plastic bags.

"Cookies are my department right now," said Mrs. Wilson, handing a bag to the woman. "But my husband here can fix iron cords, make a washing machine work, and many such things. I can baby-sit, sew on buttons, and the like. You'd be doing us a favor to let us serve you."

"Well—" said the woman hesitantly, "Well, come on in, and—"

They stayed an hour, talked, and discovered the family had five children and a piano. The man of the family had to drive forty miles to work every day and was always tired and cross when he came home. They had no church connections.

"Mrs. Mann," Mr. Wilson fairly shouted at me on the phone in his happy excitement, "the younger generation needs an awful lot of help. You were right. A boy down there does not know a monkey wrench from a screwdriver. And that neighborhood bad boy can't whittle or use a knife. I'm going to restore the lost art of whittling. And—"

Mrs. Wilson came on to say, "Those young married women don't know how to keep an orderly house—use too much washing powder in the machine and they—"

I had warned them carefully never, never to criticize: "Pour on praise! Offer help with no strings attached." Again I repeated it. I didn't need to worry. For soon the neighborhood knew the

Wilsons as part-time grandparents. They could tell stories, stay with children, walk a dog, read and play games of dominoes, checkers, and cards that no parent had time for.

Before long Mrs. Wilson was teaching some of the youngsters how to make cookies. Boys were learning from Mr. Wilson how to handle a knife and other tools. They found outlets for the energies of some of the young people in the community who had been "problem kids."

To parents worried about today's problems, Mr. Wilson listened politely and creatively, then said, "Well now, on the other hand . . ." and told them about some good thing being accomplished through the power of love at work. To some he talked about getting fresh water from ocean water. In dry California, where we depend upon irrigation ditches and pipes to bring water from hundreds of miles away, Mr. Wilson always found a ready listener as to how soon we can get a thousand gallons of fresh water from the sea for thirty cents. I gave him my copies of "Chemistry in Action," a house organ of the Truesdail Laboratories, which always is filled with brief items of good report. Mr. Wilson became a bringer of good news, hope, courage, and an optimistic look at life in the midst of discouraging daily headlines.

Then one night the Wilsons phoned me to say that tomorrow was their D-day, when they would take the driver's test before their licenses ran out. I was not surprised to hear the next day that both had passed. They had built up so much happiness and self-confidence that their whole attitude was one of success. They had a fresh store of memories of past successes and it carried them through. Once again their clock was running, ticking off one happy event after another. As we worked together awhile longer, the Wilsons paid attention to the windows in their house of love.

Becoming aware of the power of love and desiring to witness to that power, the Wilsons went on to feel that they were actually working with God, which of course they were. They asked for more written "spiritual vitamins" to use daily and to pass along when it seemed advisable. The following are some of the points of truth and love I sent them:

1. They also serve who only sit and think and pray, planting seeds of love that will bloom another day.

2. What you build into your soul growth goes with you when you go.

3. To be constantly aware of the creative power of love all around you is to keep your windows clean. This will increase your courage. *Courage is the lifter.* Courage, says Webster, is "mental or moral strength enabling one to venture, persevere, and withstand danger, fear, or difficulty firmly and resolutely." Courage is fear that has said its prayers. Courage comes from the knowledge that there is justice in the laws of God, and that God has the last word.

4. Love leads man to God and God to man.

5. Love insures growing happiness and safety now and in the future. Love is the foundation on which all civilization stands and is the next step up to which all civilization aspires.

6. The Spirit of love will still your fears, dry your tears, prolong your years, and bring you every good thing life has to offer, if you will let it.

7. Love is an open road. It always leads out and up. "Come up higher," says the Soul of the universe to the soul of man.

8. Love to witness to the power of love. Tell people, "Love is there and will take care of you, even in the turmoil of our day."

The Wilsons made a happy game of their house of love project. "We have a loose board in our floor," they would tell me. Or, "The lock on our door needs attention." They were a delight to me, two wonderful people, willing to be happy and willing to witness to the power of love to make others happy. Soon their growing was showing to themselves. And others found them becoming younger in spirit. Love always returns a compliment. The Wilsons became "part-time grandparents" of the neighborhood, and love and goodness was lavished upon them. Their cup filled to overflowing.

Here is a check list of what we have learned so far about soul growth and expansion of self-consciousness.

1. Love is the healer: love leads to action and work.
2. Work is the teacher: work leads to decisions.
3. Decision is the bridge: decision leads to prayer.
4. Prayer is the changer: answered prayer leads to love and faith.
5. Faith is the pattern-maker: faith in goodness leads to harmony of living.
6. Harmony is the joy-bringer: joy leads to self-expression and a search for law under which it can be controlled.
7. Law is the protector: knowledge of the law leads to individual courage.
8. Courage is the lifter: courage of our convictions put to work lifts us into higher consciousness and leads us to trust.

Our house of love now has four walls, foundation, floors, doors with strong locks, and windows. We've learned to love ourselves, others, God, life, goodness, harmony, the law of love, and the creative power inherent in love.

But how long would happiness dwell in a house without a roof? We are building our soul-self and expanding our self-consciousness not just for today, and today's problems. We are working as well for our eternal self and toward Christ consciousness. It will comfort us during the difficult times to remember that we will take with us all we have gained on earth.

9 Love: The Healer of Grief

LOVE THE UNKNOWN PLAN OF GOD

Trust is the comforter . . . put a roof over your house . . .
hidden and open fears . . . love is worth dying for . . . God
is a responsible Person . . . love is a North Star . . . we can't
get lost . . . God is stuck with us . . . we are stuck with God
. . . trust leads to truth.

Story from Life: The Parents Who Couldn't Forgive

> "Though he slay me, yet will I trust in him."
>
> Job 13:15

BY HANDLING OUR PROBLEMS through active obedience to the first eight parts of the law of love, we can build a house of love and develop our own integrity, wholeness, and self-consciousness. There is another need for love which, if not met, can result in the destruction of all the other eight. It is this: We must love the unknown plan of God for freewill man here and hereafter. We must be willing to be a part of it and to work with it even though the plan includes death on earth. To do this is to put a roof over our house of love.

This roof is made up of our love and acceptance of God's unknown plan because we first accept the whole love of a whole God. To work through this fact is to see how and why our first eight points of love are real, that they fit together as a whole, that none of them can be broken without loss to the others, and why love truly is the healer of every unwanted condition known to man.

So far, we have handled our problems by loving out, by building our own integrity. We passively accepted God's love. Now we need actively to accept God's love for man, which contains all the points we have been working with and more. To accept this love whether we feel worthy of it or not is to accept and trust the plan and to put the roof over our house.

At this point many people stop their housing project and live out their lives in an uncovered house. All they have gained is open to the storms of life. Of what good are foundation, floors, doors with locks, and windows when trouble comes from the area where the roof should be, as in the case of loss of a loved one in death?

This roof over our house is more than a figure of speech. It is the dividing or the connecting line between our past and future spiritual development. It concerned our ancestors and will concern our descendants. It is the connecting point between the Old and New Testaments, the key to the Christian religion, and the base of tomorrow's psychiatry, psychology, and medicine. Behind the activities of modern science is a search for God and the fate of man.

We are asking: Is God Himself whole? A mature, integrated, responsible Person? Or is He a God divided? A God of love and of hate? Of reward and punishment? Of life and death? Is He a God of all wisdom, power, and love, or does He make mistakes, leaving us at the mercy of some power greater than God—blind chance or death?

These questions have been the source of struggle, war, and fear since man began to search for God. They are contained in every system of religion, ethics, and philosophy. The Bible, understood, contains the answers. Modern science is showing many points in the Bible to be true. Psychologically and spiritually, we must put the roof over our house of love because we must have something that we believe in as good, something that stands between us and all known and unknown threats, dangers, and problems we yet will face here on earth or in any other place. We need this assurance in order to come *free from fears of the unknown.* Every fear damages us to some extent. All our lives, until we accept the perfect love of a perfect God, we entertain hidden and open fears. All our fears when carried to the extreme are contained in the fear of death ending all. Opposed to that fear is our built-in desire to live forever. "What must we do to be saved?" is the oldest cry of man. It is not death itself we fear, but what comes after. Punishment? Reward? Annihilation of nonbeingness? We fear destruction of our individual soul-self, that "house" we have been building, and destruction of our self-consciousness.

We must accept the unknown plan for man as part of God's love that serves our needs here and hereafter, or live with fear which eventually will destroy our house—our soul's wholeness, happiness, and joy in living. "A house divided against itself cannot stand." Evading the issue, never coming to grips with this question about what happens after death robs many people of health and happiness. We must accept that God is all love and that death is good and the gateway to greater living, or be troubled subconsciously all our lives. Since trust leads to truth, we shall find eventually as Job did that God is a God of love. Trying to live within the love commandments will lead us finally to trust in God.

To help you gain further insight into the above, let me tell you about the Grays, *the parents who couldn't forgive.*

That they lately had become acquainted with grief was in their eyes and manner when they came early one morning to tell me about Bill, their only child, just twenty-one, who had been killed in the Vietnam war. "We must find some kind of comfort or lose our minds," they said.

Settled in my home they poured out their hearts' questions: Why did it have to happen to Bill? Where is he now? How is he? Will we ever see him again as the radiant living person we loved? Why does God allow wars—if there *is* a God? Has the Christian religion ever worked? What *can* we believe?

They felt they could not obey the command of Jesus to love our enemies. They could not forgive the politicians, warmakers, and paid propagandists who had, with talk of freedom and righteousness equated with the Revolutionary War, incited Bill to enlist in a "Holy Cause" which was just plain murder. Bill was to have been a doctor, to have served mankind. Now, all was lost.

After listening to their recital of fears and grief and to details from Bill's letters, the message of his death, the shock of it, which was necessary for their preparation for healing, I said, "All of your questions are included in one question: Do you believe in the integrity of God? A God of all life, love, wisdom, and power, a whole and undivided God?" I explained to them that integrity means the state or quality of being complete, undivided, or unbroken; that it denotes a state of soundness, purity, also moral soundness, honesty, and uprightness.

Grief has many parts. If the Grays could trust God as whole, they could be healed of one part of their grief which was their feelings that injustice had been done. They could be healed finally of other parts of grief because trust would give them comfort and would lead them in turn to truth and to freedom from fears, doubts, and resentments. This freedom would enable them to find opportunities to make the rest of their lives more worthwhile than they had been before. The Grays were willing to learn. We talked back and forth the whole day. I started by sharing with them some of my experiences after the death of my husband in 1961. I had told them of the findings from my years of research for my book, *Beyond the Darkness*, which was my own journey into grief and the questions about what happens after death and some of the answers I found. I refer readers interested in points not covered here to that book, especially to the chapter, "Three Reasons Why I Believe We Live After Death."

The following is a composite of points the Grays and I discussed that day (not necessarily in this order) the answers they accepted, our conclusions, and some thoughts which came later as they continued to study. By points:

1. *Trust is the comforter*

Trust, according to the dictionary, is "assured reliance on another's integrity, veracity, and justice." Trust is an absolute and unquestioning resting on that which is its object and is often more instinctive than confidence, which is apt to suggest definite grounds for assurance. I believe that every human being has within himself an unkillable instinctive trust in God. In time of stress, danger, and threat to life we cry out instinctively, "My God!" for God is love, justice and mercy and wisdom beyond our present power to understand, and that is what we want at the time. The trouble comes in trying to define God. Our finite minds cannot encompass the Infinite. The Grays were not "Bible people" they said, but leaned more toward science. They needed to start with some "grounds of assurance which they could accept."

The Grays were suffering from guilt feelings, a natural part of grief common to all who love others deeply. Psychiatrist Dr. William G. Niederland, who studied 2,000 survivors of the Nazi camps, terms it the "survival syndrome." The Grays were saying, in effect, "Our son, with all his life ahead of him, and those other fine young men were taken, but we are left. It is not right."

Such a fear and sense of guilt says "God has made a mistake. He took the wrong people." Or, "God does not know or care," which is to doubt God's integrity, to doubt that He has a plan for man made of love. The Grays also felt guilty remembering mistakes they had made with Bill. This is natural, for no person has yet lived up to the full law of love. The point is that a sense of guilt ruins our faith and so our trust.

2. Love is worth dying for

The Grays, by loving Bill, fitting him for life and teaching him right from wrong, had added to the goodness of the World Soul and thereby had helped the growing consciousness and conscience of man. Their guilt was groundless. They had a right and a duty to love themselves.

Bill must have known that love is worth dying for. He loved his parents and many friends. He loved freedom and volunteered for a war he believed in. Under his free will, Bill had died for love.

3. *Neither life nor death were lost*

The experience called death cannot put out the eternal flame of life and love. They cannot be divided or cease to be. The life in man is God in man. Life either was undivided and unbroken or it was lost entirely in Bill's death. If Bill could "lose" his life in death, then a part of God could be lost with the death of every human being. If life is whole and undivided, it is so both in God and in man. Bill did not lose his life. He took it to a higher vibration of livingness. His gains are beyond our measuring, but it will comfort us to know what a scientist says about death. According to Stromberg in *The Soul of the Universe*, "The memory of an individual is written in indelible script in space-time . . . and [has] survival of memories . . . after death." And that Soul is indestructible and immortal. As an individual it has a beginning but seemingly no end. Also, "The most characteristic thing about the human Soul after it has developed a conscious-ness is its remarkable individuality and integrity." And integrity, we remember, means whole, unbreakable. Bill's life is for eter-nity.

4. *Life itself is whole*

I think life is an intelligent energy of God in the soul, a servant that must and loves to do His bidding. Life does not stop short of its purpose whether it is working on planet earth or in some other region of space. The final purpose of the unknown plan of God for man is a perfected being. God created us and is respon-sible for our welfare here and hereafter. God's wholeness, honesty, and uprightness demand it. If this were not so, the whole universe would fall apart—it would have no integrating force to hold it together. And that is exactly what love does, for it is the power that creates, works for a plan and holds things together by good purpose.

5. *If Bill is alive where is he?*

Bill is where love has placed him. Under the laws of cause and effect and of attraction and repulsion, all of which come under the law of love, Bill is now in heaven. Heaven means a state or place of pure harmony. Science says that there are billions of planets. Millions of them may be inhabited, some by beings higher than earth men. Bill went to that place with which he harmonizes, where he is in tune, comfortable and happy with his surroundings. He went to the correct schoolroom, the place where he had fitted himself to go. "In my Father's house are many mansions." Success accomplished gives joy, release, and fulfillment. Under law, Bill is happier than he ever has been before.

Bill has to be exactly where love and his own measure of soul growth placed him. I think that every living soul has a place in time and space and that our Creator God knows exactly where each soul-self is at all times, whether in or out of an earth body. Everything in the universe—star, man, or microbe—has its place, purpose, and duration. There is a love that cares, a Mind that knows every human being on earth, witnesses every hurt, joy, fair and unfair act, and impulse of hate or love and duly credits these to an individual's account, not for punishment later, but for his own good and future use. It cannot be otherwise under the law of cause and effect, which Emerson called "the Chancellors of God."

One point that worried the parental love of the Grays was whether Bill would be lost in that new world. They still feared final separation, asking "Will Bill still be Bill, and will he remember us?"

6. God is a responsible Person

Could God be aware of one lone individual soul out of the nearly four billion people on earth today? Or did Bill's soul-self simply become absorbed into a mass, as the physical body would become a part of the earth? Did Bill still have an individual consciousness? Was he still Bill? Could he remember his parents and other earth people whom he had loved? All of these questions showed that the Grays still doubted the wholeness of God and His responsibility to His created beings.

There are more cells in the human body than there are people on earth. Yet the guiding principle, the soul of the body, knows where every cell is, what it is doing and what it needs. Some doctors tell us the soul always knows how and where the body is sick. Surely it could be no problem to God to know where every individual soul He created is in space and time, what it needs, and how to supply it. God, to be God, has to be aware of every individual's thoughts, prayers, needs, and desires, here and hereafter. Keeping account would be no problem to a Mind that has created a universe run by computers of spiritual laws that work automatically. God's awareness is instant and accurate. Yes, God knows where Bill is; and Bill knows where he is and who he is, and he remembers life on earth, its people, and his parents. He is attached to them by bonds of love. Since all love is of God we can say Bill is attached to all love by love. Tomorrow science will explain how it works.

The Grays' deep grief over the way Bill died needed much help. Bill had come from a union of their bodies, their blood, their very souls and they suffered from being torn apart from part of their very selves. I explained my beliefs.

7. *Love is the North Star of the soul*

There is a homing instinct in all living creatures. Birds hatched in the far north know how and when to fly south for winter. For ages, sailors have been guided by the North Star back to home port. I believe every individual soul has this homing instinct and trusts it when it is time to leave earth school, die here, and go home again. All living things know how to go home when the time comes.

8. *They want to go*

Once the soul has left the darkness of the human body in which it was imprisoned, it finds itself in a world of light, beautiful, loving, good, and desirable—a heaven. The change is immediate. I have collected several hundred witnessed examples of "dying" people exclaiming in joy and surprise at the beauty and light they see. Jesus told the thief on the cross, "Today shalt thou be with me in Paradise." There is no waiting.

9. *How can we forgive our enemies?*

The Grays were much exercised over this point. Part of the great commandment is to love our neighbors. But Jesus said to love our *enemies* also. "Bless them that curse you, do good to them that hate you, and pray for them which despitefully use you" (Matthew 5:44). A fact the Grays had not considered was that Bill, being in war, was an enemy to the other side.

If God loves us no matter what, there must be a reason why we should love bad people for our own good. Does God love those who hurt us and our loved ones even to the death? If God is whole, unbroken, and pure love, He loves our enemies, the selfish, the greedy destroyers, those who murder, those who make aggressive warfare and those who steal, cheat, and lie to obtain a good for themselves at a loss from us. If we are to remain whole ourselves, we will have to love our enemies and forgive them for our own sake, just as God forgives and loves them.

10. *Why God forgives*

God forgives because He must, or suffer the wounds in Himself. (God is too pure to behold evil.) Not to forgive would be to "take fire in His bosom." It is part of the integrity of the Spirit of the universe, its intent and very existence, for God to be love. God forgives saint and sinner alike. He must or lose His wholeness by taking evil upon Himself. God cannot hate or desire to punish. Hate is a defense against fear. How could God fear man or anything else? How could God destroy the life he created without destroying part of Himself? Therefore, *God can only love.* It is a psychological and ethical impossibility for God to be less than whole.

We learn that forgiveness for man was set up before God created him. There came a time when man felt so sinful he could not believe God could love him, and he had to have relief from that burden of guilt. So Jesus came as a vicarious atonement for man, not that God needed it or demanded a sacrifice, but rather that man needed to believe he was "saved" by a blood sacrifice, that God loved man enough to send his Son to die for him and restore man into favor with God. Jesus proved that love was worth dying for. What we do to ourselves under the law of cause and effect is another matter. We are not punished for our sins, *but by them.*

11. *We must forgive*

We must forgive ourselves and others for the same reason that God forgives us and has no feeling for us but love. For us to hold hatred, resentment, and desire for revenge, which are defenses against fear, in our hearts and minds, is to harm ourselves even to death. It is to break up our growing Christ consciousness. Hence the teachings of Jesus to love, to forgive seventy times seven, to walk the second mile, are for the benefit of the one who has been sinned against. The reward is ours. Compensation to us is sure. It is a part of love.

12. *War and the Christian religion*

It is not up to God to stop war. It is up to freewill man to end war. When enough people understand and keep the two great commandments, war will end on earth.

We do not have to ask whether Christianity really works. We have only to read history, to look at the state of things before the coming of Christ Jesus, to learn what He taught, and to check up on what it has done for the world already, and we will know that it is the way of life that works because it is the way of love, no matter what. God can but wait until man evolves beyond war and all the other loveless acts against himself and his brother man.

The Grays worried whether they would ever see Bill again. I told them I am certain that we can't get lost. I believe that people who belong together do get together here and hereafter.

There is a guiding Person and Principle of love that sees to it. We can't get lost from love. We can trust it to the end, because it is part of God's law of progressive good for man. Such trust will lead us finally to where it led Job—to a God of love who is beyond seeing evil.

13. *We need to trust as little children of God*

We need to trust Father God (the creative principle) and Mother Nature (the feminine receptive principle, the method by which the plans are carried out) to take care of us just as little children trust loving parents to guide and care for them.

To be able to feel and to say, "Whatever death is, Father God, I accept it as good," is to accept the integrity of God the Planner and the plan. We need to trust the definite grounds of assurance also. God's plan for man has been developing through millions of years. God cares enough to do enough to see it through. We cannot see around the curve of time and cannot know what will happen next, but we can be willing for it to be so. To do this is to accept that God and His project, freewill man on earth, are good and to accept that death itself is good, as natural as birth and as needed. We are always brought back to the cause when we start to work with the effect. God's love is the cause. Death is the effect. Death is freedom from and freedom to for the individual. Death is a victory.

Death brings home to us the reason Jesus stressed so repeatedly our need to love. For only by understanding and trying to live within the two great commandments can we arrive at an emotional acceptance of God's love for us. The Grays had been trying to use reason alone. We need both mind and soul acceptance. Both the masculine and feminine sides of our nature must be satisfied and agree before we can have personal peace.

If we have given love to others with no strings attached and have received love in return, we are emotionally ready to believe that we can receive God's love here and hereafter. If we love life, how much more so does God, giver of all life, love our lives and us? If we can love good and the laws, we shall see that our first eight points of love have led us naturally to point nine—indeed, they are a part of nine.

Back and forth we talked that day, with time out for rest, food, prayers, music, and reading from the Bible or another book. By sunset the Grays had reached a working program which would enable them to study.

Before the Grays left we had a prayer service for Bill, and we lovingly placed him and his future in the care of his Father God, the original Creator and Giver of all life. We pledged ourselves anew to love, to learn and to carry on as best we might trusting God fully to care for His own. This trust finally brought peace to the Grays. They saw that God who created life must maintain it. The root must support the branch. God belongs to us and we belong to Him. We are stuck with God and He is stuck with us. There is no real purpose in living on earth or even in God's creating man in the first place, unless there is life after death.

Eventually the Grays completed their journey from the fearful belief that death is evil and no good can come of it to love of the unknown plan of God from which only good can come. Their house of love was at last completed.

PART TWO

Social and Cosmic Consciousness

To put your house of love in order to work for an environment of love and cultural advantages, produces social consciousness and leads to cosmic consciousness. A person with cosmic consciousness is one whose self-consciousness and social consciousness have expanded to a concept of his place in an orderly and harmonious universe of love and to a belief that eventually he can achieve Christ consciousness.

"There is a destiny that makes us brothers;
    None goes his way alone:
All that we send into the lives of others
    Comes back into our own."

Edwin Markham

10 Love: The Healer of Environment

LOVE THE SPIRIT OF TRUTH, FREEDOM, OPPORTUNITY

Truth is the liberator . . . our total environment . . . if we house with a cripple . . . freedom is the two-edged sword . . . liberty or death . . . freedom leads to opportunity . . . opportunity is the tester . . . invitation to greatness.

"Ye shall know the truth, and the truth shall make you free."

Jesus in John 8:23

IN PART ONE we talked about our soul-mind-self and about how to build a house of love where happiness would dwell, by keeping the first nine points of the law of love, given and implied in the two great commandments. We ended part one by learning to love and trust God's unknown plan for man. Well then, can we now just sit back and enjoy life, assured that the Spirit of happiness will continue to dwell with us ever after? No! Nothing stands still. Not even an atom. We must now maintain all we have built. If not, other forces and people can and may create such unhappy conditions that we will give up our high place and even descend into doubt and despair.

Our maintenance job will never end. There are all those other people out there who also have free will. Some of them even now are passing laws of the land under which we will have to live; some are part of the world's problems, others part of the solutions. *But all of them are part of our total environment, that place in time, space, and emotion where our house of love stands.* Our total environment is made up of all the people and things nature and man have made, plus the emotions, including

112

hate, fear, greed, and courage, and the thoughts and spoken words of yesterday and today.

A proverb says that if we house with cripples we will learn to limp. We will either learn to work with our environment and change it for the better, or it will change us for the worse. We can change it and ourselves for the better by learning and living within the final nine points of love covered in part two.

We are now ready to study point ten of the law of love.

10. *Love the Spirit of truth*

We must love the Spirit of truth because *truth is the liberator in the soul of man.* Truth has many parts, including facts found out, as by science; facts are things as they are, could be, and shall be. Truth includes the meaning of the spiritual laws and the will of God. Jesus said he had come to witness to the truth (John 18:37) and that the word of God is truth (John 17:17). Truth includes the ultimate good for man which is beyond his present wildest dreams and can be manifested only within the law of love.

Truth is the key that turns the lock that sets man free from prisons of ignorance and fear and from the unwanted results he builds by desires, thoughts, words, deeds, and feelings outside of the law of love.

Neither happiness nor love can live long in an environment of myths, mistakes, ignorance, and lies. For these breed sickness, poverty, worries, ungrounded fears, and violence that damage mind, body, and soul. Our house of love will not be secure until we have a *world-wide environment of truth.* But not all people want truth to come in. Some will struggle to hold back truth for fear of personal loss, hope of gain, or inability to accept new truth. But the thrust of truth already is affecting our established religions, philosophies, and hundreds of other parts of our daily lives.

Truth has uncovered ecological and environmental conditions that threaten the existence of all life on earth including the life of man. Truth will, I believe, bring in a great religious renaissance that will sweep the world and carry the collective intelligence and love to heights not now dreamed of. Already it is turning many to see the grim necessity for greater social and cosmic consciousness. Finally, the Spirit of truth leads to freedom.

11. *Love the Spirit of freedom*

Freedom is the two-edged sword in the soul of man. We must love the Spirit of freedom because without it man would remain as animals, ruled only by instinct and not by freewill choice and reason. One side of the sword of freedom can be used only within the law of love. The other side can be used only outside of the law of love. The love side of freedom can cut away every obstacle that stands in the way of man and his final liberty as a son of God. The loveless side cuts away the good of others for a seeming benefit to the individual who misuses it. But it finally cuts the misuser to ribbons, as ruthless dictators and individuals have learned.

Having free will, each man must choose for himself how he will use the freedom truth brings. And he will use it according to how much social consciousness he has developed. What hurts teaches. What pleases teaches. Eventually men learn to live within the law of love for the safety of all men in order not to harm themselves.

Freedom is not free. Political freedom for the individual and the nation is bought, paid for, and held by living within the laws of love, which includes "liberty and justice for all."

Today in the souls of nations over the world there is an ever-increasing struggle for freedom and rights of the individual. Every nation has a soul-self. No one could mistake the soul of England for the soul of Japan, for example, but individuals in all nations are born desiring freedom. Many new nations have been given political freedom during the past twenty-five years, but not all are doing well. A nation cannot hold freedom until it has enough citizens of soul-self-consciousness, high social consciousness, and aspirations for cosmic consciousness. It takes intelligence, self-discipline, individual responsibility, and obedience to the law of love on the nine points we have studied plus the final nine we are here looking into. Once established for the individual or the nation, freedom must be rightly used and protected. "Eternal vigilance is the price of liberty."

Freedom is not on trial. Today many fear American freedom will be lost. But in spite of the well-organized groups who seek to establish communism, the welfare state, or a dictatorship as a way of economic and environmental survival, freedom itself is not on trial. Yet all men with free will are hourly on trial for how they have used their freedom.

Emerson says that the good laws know whether we have kept them or not. Deep down in the consciousness of man is the realization that under the law of sowing and reaping, man is punished by the results of breaking the law of love.

We need a world-wide environment of freedom. When social consciousness is low and few are interested in cosmic consciousness, living only for the moment, and many break the laws of love in their use of free will and political freedom, chaos results. Rome fell in morals and the fall of the empire followed. But no matter how many individuals or nations abuse the Spirit of freedom, it yet will rule the world. Because without freedom which leads to opportunity for the individual, there is death of soul growth. And soul growth is man's purpose for being on earth. What he may be able to accomplish on some other planet is another matter.

12. Love the Spirit of opportunity

We must love the Spirit of opportunity for ourselves and others because *without opportunity we cannot fully use our God-given free will.* Opportunity means a fit time, a favorable set of circumstances for change. It is not to be confused with opportunism, which means taking advantage of something, as in politics or other circumstances, with no regard for principles or ultimate consequences. Opportunities used outside of the law of love harm the user and the human race. Opportunism uses the aggressive, not the loving side of the sword of freedom.

In souls of individuals all over the world today there is a rising cry for more livingness. There is a ceaseless demand for more opportunities to develop body, mind, and spirit. New millions now want to live in an environment of truth, freedom, beauty, peace, and security. Many are saying life must make sense, or there is no use in living. All of these good desires are children of love and cannot be obtained through force or any other power less than love at work.

Love is the healer of the moral, physical, spiritual, mental, economic, and social sicknesses of our cities, our nations, and our world; the healer of world-wide lawlessness, turmoil, and shame. Love alone can solve the problem of man against himself and man against man. There are three ways in which we can help to build a better world for all people.

A. *Set our own hearts right with God*

We must love or perish, as individuals, as a nation, as a world. Ever since Cain slew Abel, the goods of the world have been up for grabs. But no more. The harm we pour into the environment on any level comes back upon ourselves. We are not responsible for earning our brother's living, nor for forcing him to keep the law of love. But we are responsible for how we earn our own living, for how we spend our leisure and money to help others, and whether we hurt our brother in an attempt to get a good for ourselves.

B. *Guide others to use the opportunities already open to them*

This is an important work. Opportunities unused lead to failure, dependence upon others, unhappiness, sloth, bitterness, envy, and regret. Unused and misused opportunities are the source of much physical illness, mental and spiritual disturbances. To misuse life is to refuse to grow up from irresponsible children of God to responsible sons of God. We need to help others to build their own houses of love as a means of safety for all that we hold dear. This aid can also be a great source of pleasure and soul growth to the giver. Happy is the man who uses a part of his lifetime and talents to help to build a better world through better people.

C. *Work for an environment of cultural advantages in our community based on truth*

We cannot change people against their will. But we can so present the Spirit of truth, freedom, and opportunity and the fruits they bear, that people will want to change for the better. To work for and establish an environment of cultural advantages is to accept an invitation to greatness. It will help us to see how others have done this. As we read the two stories from life in our next chapter we will see *why* we must love the *Spirit of greatness*, which is point thirteen of our total of eighteen points of love.

11 Love: The Healer of the Soul of Our Cities

LOVE THE SPIRIT OF GREATNESS

Greatness is the witness . . . of supreme importance . . .
cultural satisfactions . . . worship at the shrine of beauty
. . . good is always noticed . . . one man decided . . .
greatness leads to a desire for continued learning.

Story from Life: Tale of Two American Cities

"A city that is set on a hill cannot be hid."
Jesus in Matthew 5:14

IN PART TWO we are learning how to develop social and cosmic consciousness by learning about our total environment, what we do to it, and what it does to us and to others.

Unless we love and promote the Spirit of truth, the Spirit of freedom, and the Spirit of opportunity for all, we are likely to lose what we have gained in building our own house of love. To accomplish this we need to love the *Spirit of greatness*, which is point thirteen in our eighteen points of love. This will lead us to take advantage of the cultural opportunities around us and to create and hold new ones for others. Love leads to action. If we care enough, we will do enough. Greatness is the witness to man's obedience to the will of God, which is good for all. We want to know that we are on the right track to social and cosmic consciousness. We need a place to start and a plan of procedure. The first need of every city is a moral and religious climate, an environment of truth, freedom, opportunity, and cultural advantage that leads to greatness. We need conditions that will lead to good home and family life, for with that other good will follow. This always has been the American ideal. For example:

Former President Calvin Coolidge once said that, "The foundation of all progress, of all government and all civilization, is Religion. It is only in that direction that there is hope of solution for our economic and social problems. The strength of our country is the strength of its religious convictions. Whatever inspires and strengthens the religious belief and religious activity of the people, whatever ministers to their spiritual life, is of *supreme importance*. Without it, all the other efforts will fail. With it there lies the only hope of success."

To further our own soul growth we need to help to change the soul of our own city for the better. Examples of what has been done can help us. So let me tell you the *tale of two American cities*. First, Pasadena, California.

My late husband, Herbert James Mann (an architect, engineer, artist, and musician) and I bought a home in Pasadena, because we both liked this city better than any other place either of us had lived. When we first came here in 1948, we thought it was the total surroundings of the San Gabriel Valley that appealed to us: the homes, fine public buildings, nearby San Marino's Huntington Gardens with its world-famous art gallery and library. From our patio we could see Mount Wilson, sometimes covered with snow in the winter. The Sierra Madre mountains curve from north and east and flow gently down into the great wide valley. The pictures changed with the weather but every day held beauty and inspiration. Soon we began to realize that it was the *spirit of the people*, the very *Soul of Pasadena*, that satisfied and held us.

The Soul of a city is what the people who live there have made of it, or that born of the original founders' intent and purpose which has continued to live. To know something about how the Soul of Pasadena was established and grew and where it stands today properly belongs to our studies here.

Pasadena was not a "planned" city. It began in the souls of a few extraordinary people one cold day in Indiana in the winter of 1872–73 at the home of Dr. and Mrs. Thomas B. Elliott, who were entertaining friends. They had been talking about the unusually hard winter weather and how nice it would be to live in sunny southern California. But that possibility seemed remote. Southern California was then a place of large ranches, some of them thousands of acres. Times were unsettled. The Civil War had ended not long before, in 1865. Such a venture would call for sturdy pioneers who believed in God and their own powers. Mrs. Elliott was that kind of person: "Well," she declared firmly, "I'm going to be in California next winter, whether any of the rest of you go or not."

That was an expression of deep desire, long felt, caring enough to do enough. Her powerful words of desire and decision inspired the others and set forces for success into action.

The group organized the California Colony of Indiana. In the spring of 1873 their two agents went ahead to find the best place for the colony. After many adventures and the addition of new recruits, the colony purchased part of the historic Rancho San Pasqual and organized the San Gabriel Valley Orange Growers Association. Plots were parceled out, and acres of land went to those who owned shares; groves were planted and homes started.

The founders were well-educated business and professional men with families. They were "seeking a healthy, moderate climate and cultural satisfactions." Cultural satisfactions do not grow on bushes. They are the end result of the cultural advantages which have been provided.

The Soul of Pasadena, as I see it, may be described as a desire for truth, beauty, good, and gracious living, backed up by honest, intelligent hard work. For one of the first things the colony did was to open a school, in the home of the teacher, Jeannie Clapp, with only two pupils, the Banbury Twins. There followed a regular school in 1875, the first church (Presbyterian) and the second church (Methodist) in 1877.

The name "Pasadena" was suggested by Dr. Thomas B. Elliott, which he explained meant "Crown of the Valley" in Chippewa Indian language. It was adopted in 1875 and made official by the Post Office Department in 1876. Pasadena rapidly became a tourist mecca. The spirit of the people drew like-minded settlers with money, vision, and the same desires in life. By 1880 the first hotel was built. The "elegant eighties" brought with them more hotels. Horse-drawn streetcars arrived. The stagecoaches from Los Angeles with one-day mail service gave way to a train. A land boom was soon under way, and by 1888 the population had grown to nearly 10,000. Then a recession came; many went broke; many left. But the Soul of Pasadena continued to expand and express. Then something wonderful happened.

Professor Charles Fredrick Holder, a famous writer who lived in Pasadena, organized the first Tournament of Roses, which was held New Year's Day, 1890, under the auspices of the Valley Hunt Club. Professor Holder had suggested that the people decorate their horses, buggies, and surreys with flowers grown in their own gardens and parade down Colorado Boulevard on the morning of New Year's Day, then go on to the ball park for an afternoon of games and feats of horsemanship. This venture was so successful that it was made an annual event.

Good does not long go unnoticed. A roving newspaperman saw the parade one New Year's Day when "back East" was buried in snow. His glowing story about it was copied by papers in Los Angeles, Chicago, and New York. Within five years the parade and games had become so famous, and so many people who came to see stayed that the Valley Hunt Club turned the work over to a committee of community leaders who formed the Tournament of Roses, a nonprofit association which operates the festival to this day.

The sports and contests kept pace with the Parade of Roses. The Rose Bowl was built, finally, where at one time chariot races were held. Interest in them dwindled and the Rose Bowl was used for football. It is noteworthy that the Soul of Pasadena has ruled that when New Year's Day falls on a Sunday, the parade and game are held on Monday.

These two yearly ventures have made Pasadena world-famous. But we will have missed the whole point if we fail to look behind the scenes and ask why, as we go.

People work all night before the day of the parade in a cold barn with smelly glue pots, sticking fresh flowers onto the floats. Only fresh flowers are allowed, and as many as 700,000 blossoms may be required for one large float. Many floats cost more than $30,000. Only sixty major floats are allowed, with twenty bands and two hundred thoroughbred horses. Some twelve hundred persons ride or march in the musical units. Men wait in line for years for the opportunity and honor of working for the association without pay. The Rose Bowl Queen and her six princesses are chosen from competing Pasadena schoolgirls. A Rose Queen has been chosen every year since 1905. Grand Marshals of the parade have included the Reverend Billy Graham and President Dwight D. Eisenhower. The work of getting the parade and the game together involves thousands of people who happily invest their time, energies, love, money, and skills in these two ventures. Why?

Why do millions of people watch on television the two-hour, six-mile Tournament of Roses parade? And why do more than a million and a half people, coming from everywhere, line the streets of Pasadena—standing, sitting on camp stools, perching on ladders or atop parked cars and trucks, leaning out of office building windows, filling the high-priced grandstand seats—wait happily, noisily, good-naturedly, and expectantly hours before the parade starts? Hundreds camp on the streets all night to ensure a good viewing spot, and some have not missed a parade in thirty years.

Why? Because man naturally worships at the shrine of beauty, truth, good, and gracious living. He loves greatness and the "cultural satisfactions," whether he admits it or not, or whether he is envious or angry that others have it and he does not. Even when he destroys the beauty that others have created he cannot kill God's Spirit within him. And the Tournament of Roses reminds the viewer that all life on earth can be better than it ever has been for anyone. Viewer and participator are joined in an act of worship.

From the first note of the heralder's trumpet, the viewer becomes emotionally involved. The trumpet tells him that this New Year could be better than last year. It is a sign of high hope that brings unashamed tears.

Hope is a deep desire with expectations of fulfillment. And every human heart has a hope of better and greater living. As the beauty, the color of the floats with their millions of fresh, bright flowers, their load of happy human beings dancing, singing, clowning, passes before him, the viewer is transported into a land of magic. His heart takes up the happy beat and rhythm of the marching bands; the spirit of marching youth—the pretty baton-twirling majorettes strutting with the joy of life—involves him in greatness of living. He is more than he was before.

Then the sight of the horses, heavy silver trappings glistening in the sun, the obviously happy owner-riders, the ringing sound of horseshoes on pavement, carry the viewer farther and farther into the land of dreams where freedom abounds and life is always good. He knows instinctively that the whole world should be full of happiness, romance, laughter, gaiety, music, color, beauty, and acts of true unselfishness between members of the human race for a common good. Even though it is only a temporary environment of high happiness it is worth all he pays to be a part of it.

In the afternoon at the Rose Bowl, more than one hundred thousand persons, joined by another eighty million around the world through television, come more alive as they watch human beings, not killing each other, but playing together in sport, in earnest contesting fairly and honorably against each other, for fun, excitement, and great livingness.

For one wonderful day the viewer has lost the sense of care, loneliness, and smallness of his workaday world. He has been involved emotionally, mentally, spiritually, and socially in largeness, in the sharing of good and gracious living as a child of God should. He is a better human being for having experienced something divine and he knows it. And even though he might not be able to articulate the fact, his soul has grown a little higher, his self-consciousness has expanded a little further toward social and cosmic consciousness. He is a bigger and better person. He has new hope for tomorrow.

Has this double venture paid off through the more than eighty years running? The whole San Gabriel Valley says yes. People start to arrive right after Labor Day for the winter season. The Rose Bowl is known the world over as "the grandfather of all football bowl games." The Rose Bowl has won some historic firsts. In 1929 for the first time in history a game was carried over transcontinental radio. Nineteen fifty-two marks the first game by television into homes. In 1968 color coverage began, carried by satellite to Hawaii and the South Pacific. Has it paid off? Ask the advertisers who buy the TV and radio time. Or try to get a seat for the next New Year's Day game and remember the cost of parking and all the spending you'll do happily while there. Ask the flower growers; ask anyone who participates.

But what of the everyday living in Pasadena? This city, only 22.5 square miles in area, is a giant in the results of its continued search for truth, beauty, and good, gracious living and opportunities for the individual, backed up by intelligent, honest, hard work. The cultural satisfactions its founders wanted today include the following:

The California Institute of Technology, with its related Jet Propulsion Laboratory, birthplace of the United States space age, helped to put the first men on the moon in July 1969 and all those since. There are many public and private schools and colleges; night schools and adult education classes are crowded. Roughly one-third of the Pasadena male population and one-fifth of the female population are college graduates.

Mount Wilson Solar Observatory has the second largest telescope in the world. There are almost two hundred churches, and a public library is within walking distance of every home in Pasadena. The Civic Auditorium brings the best to the West. At this time a block-large convention center is being built. There is a new art museum, and new stores, office buildings, apartments and homes are being built. There are flower shows, art exhibits, and at Christmas the nightly lighted Christmas Tree Lane and blocks of neighborhood decorations from the hills through the valley. Added to this are lectures, conventions, courses, and hundreds of organizations, large and small, dedicated to the cultural advantages required and supported by the Soul of Pasadena. About 15,000 students attend Pasadena City College. Anyone who knows Dr. Armen Sarafian, President of City College and a lifelong Christian, knows of the ideals and plans he has and what already has been accomplished in the college. I am convinced that some of the youth there today will help to give us a better world tomorrow. They are not just self- and local-minded. They are social- and cosmic-minded.

"And is Pasadena still perfect in these troubled days?" someone may ask. "I have heard it said that. . . ."

Well, just now we neither look nor smell like a rose all over. Crime and other problems are on the increase. We have hippies, unhappies, alcoholics, divorces, lawbreakers and a wide assortment of spiritual infants bawling, fighting, and demanding more and more good that they have not earned, refusing to take advantage of the good they could have by working for it. Many citizens have left town for smogless skies elsewhere, or lower taxes, or to avoid the political situation, desegregation of schools, and streets torn up for new freeways. Even the great Pasadena College of the Nazarene Church, a few blocks from my home, has announced it has bought a new home in San Diego and its campus is up for sale. Yes, we have problems with new ones coming up daily.

For the record, people keep reminding each other that we have eighty-six school buses in operation to transport approximately 12,500 schoolchildren in a desegation program which adds pollution to the air, causes anger in many parents and teachers, and creates more bills for the taxpayer. Both blacks and whites are unhappy. In the past two years school enrollment has dropped by 3,550. Meetings are being held. Some want to throw the whole program out. Others want to keep it as it is. Recent elections show a new determination to solve Pasadena's problems.

Recently a captain on the Pasadena police force for twenty-two years came to the First United Methodist Church, of which I am a member, to tell us about crime and vice in our city. Pasadena is now one of the worst in the United States for its size. Pasadena is currently said to be no longer a charming, restful, sedate center for visiting tourists. The city today is comprised of individuals from many ethnic groups. Fifty-four percent of the schoolchildren are nonwhite.

Many think that Pasadena will continue to go down. But I am firmly convinced that there are enough people here who are so well grounded in the desirability of truth, beauty, and gracious living, with greater freedom and opportunity for individual soul growth, that the *Soul of Pasadena will hold and bring good out of evil*. Since 1971, Pasadena *has* greatly improved. And I predict that the Soul of Pasadena will continue to hold and take us to greater and greater heights as the city starts its second 100 years. I am convinced that all this turmoil and change and strong feelings form the ground from which genius will arise. In a high school near my home there are Armenian, Chinese, Japanese, Italian, Black, Spanish and old-line-white American boys and girls. Their activities show they are loaded with potential good for Pasadena and the world.

No one, to my knowledge, has yet started a California Sweet-Smelling Violet Society in Pasadena. But it would not surprise me to hear of one tomorrow. And if no one else does, I, being a dues-paying, card-carrying member of the Pasadena Historical Society and of the Pasadena Beautiful Foundation, might just start one myself! I expect to live here the rest of my life, and it is incumbent upon me to do what I can to add to the cultural satisfactions of this city I so dearly love.

"Oh," someone might say, "Pasadena got a head start nearly a hundred years ago. No city could change what it is now, or set up such a city-soul today."

No? Let me cite as another example of high soul-self and social consciousness at work, Steeleville, Illinois, a farming community with a population of about 2,000.

One John Steele, a farmer from Tennessee, was the first settler there, arriving about 1807. The town was incorporated in 1888. In 1890, the same year that Pasadena held its first Tournament of Roses, a man in Steeleville was given permission to use the city park for pasturing his sheep. Things went along routinely through the years until 1965, when *one man*, Dr. M. A. Ivanuck, in his second term as mayor, decided to *do* something.

We always express our soul-self, that which we are and have become through obedience to, or flouting of, the laws of love. Dr. Ivanuck, an ardent lover of nature, felt that community development should include beautification, and that Steeleville should become the flower capital of southern Illinois. This man loved life and the laws of nature, order, and beauty, for he had a high social consciousness and appreciated their value. He put his love to work. He planned for a beautification project to include a flowerbox the length of the city park. The plan was adopted by his board of trustees and implemented in 1965.

Dr. Ivanuck ran into a lot of opposition. There are always those who drag their feet instead of running to meet a new good. Some said sidewalks and street improvements were needed instead. But Dr. Ivanuck got the flowerbox, built of stone, about 360 feet long, and filled it with flowers by early spring of 1966. First there were tulips, with petunias right behind them, planted by Dr. Ivanuck himself with the help of one other man. After the tulips were finished, chrysanthemums were planted behind the petunias, so that there would always be flowers in Steeleville. About November, the mums were removed to make way for Christmas decorations. The project was a blooming success.

In 1967, Dr. Ivanuck increased his efforts. He appointed a beautification commtitee of public-spirited men and women which included Katie Fine, columnist of the town newspaper. Many volunteered help. The town gave away 1,500 petunia plants and the whole community thought petunia. By July the many-colored petunias bordered lawns, fences, and walks and flourished in redwood boxes in the business district. They bloomed at the foot of the old water tower, a town landmark, and the old bandstand came in for a renovation. The Chamber of Commerce and businessmen and women all worked together.

Did Project Petunia attract attention? My first notice of it came from my sister Fredia Nordberg, also a writer, who then lived in southern Illinois. She heard such colorful reports that she went to see and wrote an article about it for a national magazine. My other sister, Ina Gibson, who lives near Steeleville, sent me clippings about it.

Little Steeleville, which always had a Fourth-of-July celebration, was selected as the place to celebrate the big sesquicentennial (150 years) of statehood for Illinois on Independence Day 1968. People came from all over. Dignitaries and politicians, including a British and a French consul, as well as a representative of the State of Virginia, and many other people of high social consciousness, people big enough to love beauty, crowded into the place. There was a parade with bands and floats, a beauty queen, a picnic; but best of all that 360-foot long box of blazing petunias stopped the traffic.

Dr. Ivanuck had an eye to the future. He felt that "a visitor to an area gains his first impression from the general appearance. If he gets from the physical appearance of things the feeling that local inhabitants care about their city, then he is likely to expect them to care about him as a visitor. He may be interested in settling in the town or perhaps in locating some industry there."

Unlike many other small towns all over the United States, Steeleville is not losing population. It has put love to work. I believe that no one can look upon beauty and not be the better for it, and that all of us could improve the souls of our cities.*

---

* I am indebted for most of this material to Dorothy Ivanuck, wife of Dr. Ivanuck, for her letters and for her answers to my many questions by letter and in person when I visited her in Steeleville in October 1972. And also for the packet of beautiful color photographs, "Flowers of Steeleville," and "Our Proud City" greeting cards. This project has developed into an annual event.

12 Love: The Healer of Ignorance

LOVE TO LEARN

*Learning is the path . . . wisdom is the reward . . . peace is
the goal . . . poise is the stabilizer . . . power is the tempter
. . . new mansions of the soul . . . thirst for knowledge is
here to stay . . . cosmic consciousness leads to a desire to
live forever.*

"Happy is the man that findeth wisdom."
Proverbs 3:13

IN PART ONE we learned to build our house of love, our soul-mind-self, where happiness would dwell. We learned to love ourselves, others, life, God, goodness, harmony, the law of love, the creative power of love, and God's unknown plan for man.

In part two we are learning about our total environment, the place in time and space and the emotional climate in which our house stands. We have seen that we must add good, and only good, to that environment. To protect ourselves from the bad in it we need to love the Spirit of truth, freedom, and opportunity and to promote cultural advantages that lead to greatness in the individual.

To accomplish our goals we need to *love to learn.* This movement in consciousness has five parts. Properly carried out they will lead us to cosmic consciousness. And as we work toward cosmic consciousness, we will soon realize that guidance is being presented to us without our asking. Because today, in the Soul of the universe, there is a drawing closer of God, the Creator and man the created in an ever-increasing awareness of their relationship.

In our last chapter we finished point thirteen of our need to love in our total of eighteen, which was to love the *Spirit of greatness*, which led to a desire for continued learning. Now we go on with point fourteen.

14. *Love to learn forever*

We must learn to love forever, because *learning is the path the individual soul must take to find God.* God never makes a mistake. The whole universe is foolproof. We are destined to become more and more willing and able to create good and only good. All other ways fail. Jesus taught that there is no way to break through and steal the good that man is born desiring and that has been set up for man from the beginning. Our need is to build a cosmic consciousness which will finally lead us to Christ consciousness. It takes both the feminine quality of the soul and the masculine quality of the mind to grow toward a whole, perfect being, a complete self. This can be done only within the law of love.

Our modern world-wide troubles show us why the human race must love to learn and learn to love. For where there is ignorance there is often sickness, poverty, and suffering. These conditions create frustration and fear, and fear creates hate as a defense. Hate and fear create a high energy which must find an outlet. This is often blind rage, war, crime, violence, and destruction. We cannot make our own lives worthwhile as long as others are bound and threaten us. So we must love to learn and teach the truth that frees. There is no other way for man to survive. Every man is now within the range of the other man's anger and guns. Everything contrary to the two great commandments is contrary to the Spirit of learning, the truth that sets man free. *Learning leads to wisdom.*

15. *Love wisdom*

We must learn to love wisdom because *wisdom is the reward of continued love and learning.* Wisdom is insight, the ability to judge life and facts. Wisdom is stored learning, the accumulated parts of truth; wisdom is knowing that God is not mocked, that spiritual laws cannot be broken.

When we build up to wisdom we become valuable and powerful broadcasters of invisible good for our total environment by our thoughts, feelings, and desires under love. Fifty years ago Charles Fillmore, co-founder of the Unity School of Christianity, taught that our thoughts can parch the earth and bring on drought and famine. Today science has added much proof of this truth. *Wisdom leads to peace.*

16. *Love peace*

We must learn to love peace because *peace is the earth goal of the individual man and of the human race.* Peace is that state of consciousness that knows no hurt and feels no need to give hurt. At the Last Supper Jesus said, "Peace I leave with you, my peace I give unto you; not as the world giveth, give I unto you (John 14:27).

The world thinks money, prestige and security will bring peace. Nothing less than living within the law of love and continued learning can ever bring or maintain peace in a man's soul. We cannot break the law of love in any degree without doing some soul-mind-self damage to ourselves and our peace. It should be our goal to achieve the peace Jesus knew. His peace was the result of his utter conviction that God's unknown plan for man is pure love and that man has nothing to fear. To attain such peace enables us to work quietly and well with the current problems in our daily lives.

If we love peace we will work for it in our total environment. Only with permanent worldwide peace can we build heaven on earth. Everything contrary to the two great commandments is contrary to the Spirit of peace. Our practice should be to stop all inward, silent, secret, and all open hostilities toward ourselves, others, God, and the plan. *Peace kept leads to poise.*

17. *Love poise*

We must learn to love poise because *poise is the stabilizer.* When we enter this new area of high consciousness, we generally stay there for some time in a state of balance, in which we are sure about ourselves, life, others, and God at least fifty-one percent of the time. Problems will still come. Some days we are more than fifty-one percent successful. We go up and down. Finally, this state of poise holds more than fifty-one percent of the time. We soon become aware of unlimited power waiting for us out there as we work consciously and steadily toward it. Any infraction of the law of love will break up our power to some degree. As we approach the end of point seventeen, we are heading for the greatest test of our lifetime in using our free will. *For poise leads to creative power.*

18. *Love spiritual, mental, creative power*

We must love, understand, and use with caution the creative power because *power is the tempter.* Creative power is the ability to act for a predetermined purpose. This power has no conscience, no purpose, no plan. These lie in the will of the person who uses it.

Power leads man to the crossroads in his life. A feeling of power leads to an urge to control others for one's own benefit, at their expense and effort, or to an urge to help others at one's own expense and effort. It is the dividing line in our soul-mind-self in growth. Under love, power gives us the urge to help, to become as gods. Outside of love, under compulsive greed or ruthlessness, power tempts us to become as devils. The choice is ours.

This sense and sureness of great power over conditions and other persons is the most trying temptation that man experiences on earth. All must go through it to some degree. Not even the Lord Jesus was spared. He refused to use the power to try to own and control the world. He ordered Satan (temptation) to depart. Each one of us will have to make that decision for or against the law of love.

Some of my students have progressed until they came to a point of tremendous power. It releases a kind of fury of energy, daring, desire, and plans. It sharpens the mind and wit even to cunning. "I see how I can get one million dollars," one man told me. It was a way that broke the law of love, but he "could not stop the insane driving," as he later described it. He fell from his high place and had to start over with point one, learning to love himself.

When we have overcome the temptation to use our tremendous power for evil and firmly decide to use it for good and only for good, we start to rise in consciousness. We will experience to some degree what Jesus experienced. Angels will come to minister to us. This means unseen help, higher ideas, expanded consciousness, peace, poise, and often new friends to help us. From then on the individual is aware that he is indeed working toward cosmic consciousness. No one knows how far the human mind can go, because no one knows the ultimate capacity of man's ability and willingness to love and so to let God's mind work through him. Job spoke of the "glorious liberty of the sons of God" and Jesus said that we would learn to do the works he did "and greater works." Modern science is bringing us closer and closer to the great truth about man, that he has unlimited power to create directly with his mind and spoken word. But without love guiding the activities, the individual will fall eventually even from heaven itself. Hence Jesus taught the law of love as a control over creative power of the mind and individual desires.

This point of power, the eighteenth, brings to an end the series of steps in love we have taken. From that high plateau we begin a new series of eighteen steps. If we have decided for love in using our power, we begin a new series with a sense of love of our self as we did in part one. It is a great and humbling experience that brings gratitude and joy to the student, because he is meek and teachable. It brings ecstasy to the soul-mind-self. This is the state that some drug-takers are trying to experience, but they cannot achieve it this way. We can't break through and steal.

From there on each of the series of eighteen steps is on a higher plane of cosmic consciousness. Our happiness and joy in living can no longer be contained in such small quarters as we first built. So we start to build a mansion with our cosmic consciousness. Such learning leads to a desire to live forever and a sure knowledge that we can and will. Our new house of love will be easier to construct than our first one was. For now we know that "except the Lord build the house, they labor in vain that build it" (Psalm 127:1).

We started out simply in our journey into learning, but from the first we were reaching for the stars of understanding of love and how to use our free will to reach great heights of accomplishment, joy, and happiness.

How much have we learned? We will benefit greatly by taking a test.

PART THREE

Three Self Tests

Knowledge is power only if used. To test your soul-self-consciousness and your social consciousness, put them to work to help to build a better world through better people. To test your cosmic consciousness, face the worst that could happen and be willing for it to be so.

"Be ashamed to die until you have won
some victory for humanity."

Horace Mann

13 Put Your City on a Hill

LOVE YOUR CITY

Write the three stories of your life . . . be somebody special
. . . give beauty for ashes . . . leave your light on.

ONE OF THE DIRECTIVES I write in my students' notebooks is this: If you have no plan for success you are planning to fail.

At this point in our studies, the earnest reader will want to take a test of what he has learned so far. He can do this by using the two charts following chapter fourteen and comparing them with his own life. He should write out the three stories of his life: where I was, where I am, and where I want to go. He should also ask himself the questions I ask my students as given in part one, but especially: Where does it hurt? What do I want changed? What would it take to make me happy? What do I want to pray about? This should be followed by the mirror test.

Having done this the student is ready to test his social consciousness. He can do this by reading the directives that follow on how to put your city on a hill. It is not to be taken lightly. It is a practical project that the earnest student, the one who wants a better world for himself and others, should carry out.

In the May 1972 issue of the Thomas Jefferson Research Center *Bulletin*, Founder and President Frank Goble wrote: "Most American cities are in serious trouble. The continuing increase in crime, delinquency, vandalism, illegitimacy, divorce, venereal disease, and alcohol and drug addiction, which we have been reporting on a national basis, is repeated statistically in virtually every city." In this article Goble gives hair-raising facts of how increased crime and other abuses have increased taxes. The responsible reader is left wondering what he can do. He had better do something, for all he has and holds dear (the house we have been building included) is in danger. There *is* something you can do: you can *put your city on a hill.*

If you will build into the people of your city a high social consciousness of law, order, truth, beauty, honesty, justice, mercy, great livingness, and the need for individual soul growth —parts of the law of love—they will become the light of the whole community and all who come in contact with it. So be somebody special; let your light shine; become a part of history by putting to work the truth we've been learning here. Some practical points on how to put your city on a hill are as follows:

1. *Give your city the mirror test*

Take a walk or drive through your city with notebook and camera and record what you see. Visit your city hall, jail, court, police department, schools, libraries, fine homes, parks, and the slum section if there is one. Count up influences good and bad. Learn how many are on welfare and what is being done to help them to help themselves. Is it truth, love, and honesty at work, or questionable, needless, and costly political expediency?

2. *Take a case history of your city*

What is the Soul of your city? How was it first established—by what kind of people and for what purpose? What are its present goals? As you go from your home to work or shop, does your city build up your spirit or tear it down? What in your city feeds your natural hunger for freedom, soul growth, happiness, peace of mind, and beauty? Don't be afraid of the bad you find. Truth used leads to freedom, and freedom leads to opportunity. Where there is a will to good there is a way to good. In facing the truth about your city remember truth includes good that could and should be done.

3. *Ask yourself some questions*

Is there anything unlovely or unwanted in your city that finds a reflection in your own soul-self? Do you vote? Belong to a church and attend regularly? Attend night classes of any kind? Belong to a service club? Do volunteer work? Do you agree that a city exists for the benefit of its citizens and that the citizens themselves are responsible for the state of affairs in their city?

4. Take a firm stand

If your city is already on a hill of high consciousness of good, you need only to work with it for an ever-expanding growth in good. If it leaves much to be desired; then take a firm stand to make changes. Righteous indignation is love at work. That which one tolerates, one likes. That which any human being decides is intolerable is immediately changed. First in mind, then in action, then in fact. Don't leave it to the politicians, the subdividers, the freeway builders, the urban-renewal planners, or the state or federal government agencies. None of these groups are organized for your individual soul growth. Plan your work; then work your plan.

5. Come to a decision

Out of the many things that might need to be changed for the better, select only one at first and work it out in your own mind and on paper. Classify your solution: will it meet the mental, physical, moral, and spiritual needs of the citizens? Is it love at work, or an attempt at force? Love in action always gives greater freedom from or freedom to all concerned. The better you understand what it is you want accomplished, the quicker you will find the means to implement your plan and like-minded people to work with you.

6. Call for help

Start with prayer. When your project can be stated in one sentence you are ready to talk to others. Find one person to agree with you and go on asking for help. Together set up a nonprofit organization and continue to ask others to join you.

7. Keep your courage high

Courage is faith that has said its prayers. Faith is a belief that the best will come. Every new idea meets with opposition, especially if enough people are making money from the situation that needs to be changed. Remember that your cause is just. A better city means better people. Better people build a better city. Keep your circle enlarging and moving. Love always works in a circle for the good of all concerned.

8. Get your project talked about—favorably

Pasadena's Tournament of Roses caught on like wildfire after a newspaper had spread the word far and near. And the Steeleville Project Petunia took hold when a newspaper columnist began to whip up interest and an article was published in a national magazine.

9. Include beauty in your project

According to Webster, beauty is that "quality or qualities of a person or thing which give pleasure to the senses and pleasurably exalts the mind or spirit. Also, physical, moral, or spiritual loveliness; as, the beauties of nature." Continued worship of beauty will create a city so clean, comfortable, safe, beautiful, friendly, orderly, and inspiring that it will help everyone in it to grow in consciousness of good. There will be music, happiness, joyous self-expression, learning, law, order, places of recreation, and high real-estate values. Love at work creates an environment that makes real estate valuable and attracts new, good people who are willing to pay for cultural advantages.

10. Expand your plans as you go

There are some 1,200 cities in the United States that have some kind of annual celebration in which the whole community is involved. If your project gives truth for lies, beauty for ashes of riots or burning hatreds, help for indifference, then the Spirit of love will move it along and others will help to keep it going.

11. *Start right where you are*

Every community in America could use a city-betterment or city-beautiful organization. We need cities where no adult drives carelessly, where there are no children in jail and none out of school.

12. *Give your city a slogan*

San Francisco has built fame on its slogan, "The City That Knows How." If your slogan expresses love at work, you will have a surefire winner. Your slogan might be "Your City Cares How," with lists of the things your city cares about to improve human life and happiness. Hold a contest to select a slogan. The more people who hear about your plan the more will want to become a part of it.

One person can start it. One woman started Hollywood Bowl with its music under the stars, now past its sixtieth famous year. Love always leaves an imprint. If you care enough to do enough you will become a part of your city's history. You will not be here forever. But do your work today and tomorrow's people will say of you that you have gone out (passed from this life), but you took care to leave your light on, meaning you left a good work that will live on after you have gone.

14 Love: The Healer of War

LOVE BRAVERY

But what if? . . . test for cosmic consciousness . . . fear is a large part of our environment . . . be willing for it to be so.

". . . When all else has fallen."
Paul in 1 Corinthians 13:8

OUR CHAIN OF GROWTH in cosmic consciousness is no stronger than its weakest link. The question is, can we face the worst that could happen, be willing for it to be so, and still believe in God to bring us through? Learning about the way of life that works is all very well and good, but what if the world *is* blown up? Fear is a large part of our environment. Today many people believe that the end of the world is near, that the human race is about to become extinct. It could happen, either by the slow way, a do-it-ourselves job, or the quick way, the bomb. Let's look at both.

The slow way to end the world is through continued internecine strife. This method of contention for superiority through altercation, conflict, and deadly struggle born of selfishness, ignorance, fear, and greed at work if continued can, and doubtless will, lead to a total moral, physical, mental, and spiritual breakdown. It has many parts of human activity: overpopulation, continued pollution, adulterated food, smoking and excessive drinking, drug abuse and lack of self-discipline. The national habit is now to take a pill for every ill and to refuse all self-discipline. Millions are encouraged in this moral breakdown by competing pressure groups who have goods to sell. These four ways of total breakdown of all life on earth are working all over the world today. They are the results of the lack of love and learning. It is entirely possible for man to wreck planet earth and himself. We still have a choice.

In considering the quick ways to extinction, there is an age-old fear that God will destroy the world. A biblical prophecy says that man will become so evil that two-thirds of the world will be destroyed, and but for the sake of the "elect," all would be destroyed. The biblical scholar Thomas Troward says this could happen, just as the Flood happened, and for the same reason. Man seems to want to punish himself, to expiate his sense of guilt from wrongdoing. The story of the Flood could have been a mental and spiritual cleansing. Biblical scholars say that the Flood was brought on because people had become so wicked, sinful, and evil that they no longer could control the evil forces they had created. They wanted to stop the evil but were power-less to do so. Water in the Bible often means consciousness. Biblical scholars think man himself brought on the Flood. The need was for a new start to cleanse the mind, soul, and body.

The Bible says that the next great destruction of earth will be by fire. This could mean the bomb. The fear of total extinction by war I call the Hiroshima syndrome. The world is not going to forget that bomb. The Soul of Germany developed a Hitler. The Soul of Russia raised up a Stalin. Mao came up out of the soul of China's warlords. Japan, controlled by the soul of conquest, tried to conquer China and later had a try at the United States at Pearl Harbor. America perfected the atomic bomb, which is known to the world. The Russian communists and the Chinese imperialists could come to grips, and the rest of the world could go down in their death struggle for supreme controlling power of the world. It *could* happen.

On the other hand, destruction by fire may mean a holy zeal for love and perfection of man that will burn out every impurity and desire for evil in the mind and soul of man. This would destroy the world as it is and bring the old order of fear, hate, revenge, compulsive greed, and lust for power over others to an end. Through love we could bring in that new heaven on earth which we discussed in the Message to the Reader. It *could* happen.

I believe there will be no blowup, no slowup; but instead the world of man is in for a great growup. The individual will come into something bigger, something better, something more than any individual ever had before on earth. All the old methods of war power, hate power, and power politics are on the way out. The soul and mind of man have simply outgrown them. We will see new millions talking about and starting to live the golden-rule way of life. Here are some reasons why I think we are going straight ahead, safely, sanely, and happily.

1. *God is not mocked*

God will have the last word. Creative Spirit does not stop short of fulfillment of its plan.

2. *God loves us, no matter what*

Man, as man, has been on earth only about 200,000 years. That is a very short time when we consider that it takes billions of light-years for the light of some stars to reach planet earth. Light travels at 186,000 miles per second. Figure the seconds in a year, in a billion years, and see how far we are from the stars which God created. Our earth was once part of a star. We are in fact, "stardust eaters.'" Man must be more important than a star.

3. *The world is worth saving*

Planet earth is a good-sized parcel of real estate. It took billions of years to turn it into a fit habitation for man. Scientists, such as A. Cressy Morrison, have shown how exactly fitted it is to the needs of man. Its perfect plan and specifications were carefully prepared. God must be aware of the value of His property. He must be interested in His tenants and know whether they are tearing up the place or keeping it in good repair. A wise landlord gives the good tenant an extra chance if he falls into difficulties.

4. *People are worth saving*

We see the love and nobility in "ordinary people" when extraordinary threats abound, as during the terrible forest fires set by vandals in southern California in the late summer of 1970. And after earthquakes or other disasters anywhere in the world people rush to give help. The seed of God in man always springs forth when called upon. During the last two thousand years the World Soul and the Soul of the universe have been receiving vibrations of love from man which fall back to earth and impregnate our invisible invironment, the soil, water, and trees and the minds of people. This force may seem to slumber, but it comes furiously awake when the human race is threatened. We rush to put out the fire that would extinguish us. We know instinctively that man was born to live, not to die; born to grow to distinction, not to die in extinction.

5. *There are enough good people in the world to save it*

Personally, I am proud of earth's people who are working, learning, and loving their way to higher goals. I am proud of my fellow Americans and of my generation—the grandparent set. Our children and grandchildren will top us and bring in a better world for all people. More than 90 percent of modern youth are sound. Some of the spoilers are those who want a better world but see no way to get it. They are striking at people instead of at principles. But the "good kids" will tell it to the others "like it is." Youth learns from youth.

6. *Love is greater than hate*

Love is the mightiest force in the world and that's where we live. If enough people could generate enough love, we could swing the balance to safety and progress right now! How many are enough? Let me tell you. It will make you feel ten years younger and two feet taller! Einstein said that if 2 percent of the people decided that there should be no more war, that there could be no more war. Two percent of the people could stop

war? Yes. It has been shown that only 2 percent of the Commu-
nist leaders control all the others which is said to be two-thirds of
the people on earth. That 2 percent of peace-minded and peace-
determined people actually exist and are rapidly seeking and
finding each other and are working to end war forever.

"Oh, but time is running out!" someone may say. All right, let's
admit our fears and look at what would happen if the quick way
of blowing up the world should come. What if man, with gun in
hand, hate, fear, and greed for power and control in heart, starts
the war that will finally blow up the world?

First, let us remember that not even a sparrow could fall without God's permission and the use of God's power and laws. If
destruction comes; then God will have allowed it through honor-
ing man's free will. Then what?

Jesus said that the world would pass away (he did not say
when), but he did say that *his words would not pass away*. Then
all that he taught would still hold true. Blowing up the world
would not be the end of man. Life is forever and is not in the
keeping of man. A bomb cannot end life. We would wake up on
the other side and someone would be sure to sigh and say,
"We know now that way of life fails. We can't go blasting ourselves to success and happiness and a better world." And someone else surely would add, "If only we had tried to live within
the law of love." A third person doubtless would quote the words
of the two great commandments.

But what will become of us then? God, having made planet
earth and us, knows our needs before we ask. So out there in
God's territory of billions and billions of stars, there must be
one fit and ready for God's children who tore up their own
planet. Loving earth fathers are known to replace the torn up
toys of their children and rebuild houses when needed. We will
be at home wherever God sends us. And His love will be there,
waiting, even if we have not taken much love with us. And
where there is God's love, there is every good thing the heart of
His created being could want. His mental, spiritual, physical,
and emotional needs will be met. God's plan is foolproof.

7. *Love is here to stay*

One of the helps I suggest to my students who fear the end of things is to read 1 Corinthians, 13:1–8 once a week until healed of that fear. First to read it from the King James version for the deep beauty, poetry, and music of it. Then to ask himself which of today's world problems with its threat of extinction of man would remain if enough people lived within the law of love and kept the two great commandments. Not one! So let us now come to the conclusion of this whole matter by reading 1 Corinthians 13:8 in the J. B. Phillips version, which renders Paul's words as follows: "Love knows no limit to its endurance, no end to its trust, no fading of its hope; it can outlast anything. It is, in fact, the one thing that still stands when all else has fallen."

Love will outlast anything!

Of course. Love is the nature of God. And God is forever. Since we as individuals have the seed of God in us; then we also were made to last forever.

So what's to cry? Nothing.

We need to take a hitch in our courage, to love the bravery of others, to daily put our own house of love in order, to work daily for the betterment of our total environment, and to get ready to build more stately mansions for our own soul-mind-self.

The place to start is right where we are, to keep the law of love. That great new age that always has been carried in the heart of man will come in. God has a plan for man. It is good. It will work. If not on this planet, then on another. Love is here to stay, and let us constantly remember that love always leads to work.

So let us do our level best and cheerfully leave to God the rest.

Reference Charts for the Reader

BUILD A LADDER

Heaven is not gained at a single bound;
   But we build the ladder by which we rise
   From the lowly earth to the vaulted skies,
And we mount to its summit round by round.
Josiah Gilbert Holland

15 How You Work

BUILD A LADDER OF LOVE

THE 18 POINTS OF LOVE WE HAVE STUDIED:

1. Love yourself.
2. Love others.
3. Love life.
4. Love God.
5. Love inherent goodness.
6. Love the harmony of life.
7. Love the law of love.
8. Love the creative power of love.
9. Love the unknown plan of God.
10. Love the Spirit of truth.
11. Love the Spirit of freedom.
12. Love the Spirit of opportunity.
13. Love the Spirit of greatness.
14. Love to learn forever.
15. Love wisdom.
16. Love peace.
17. Love poise.
18. Love the creative power of the mind.

16 What You Accomplish

BUILD A LADDER OF SOUL AND MIND
GROWTH. THIS ALSO INCLUDES GROWTH
AND CONTROL OF EMOTIONS.

1. Love is the healer: love leads to action and work.
2. Work is the teacher: work leads to decisions.
3. Decision is the bridge: decision leads to need of prayer.
4. Prayer is the changer: answered prayer leads to love and faith.
5. Faith is the pattern-maker: faith leads to harmony of living.
6. Harmony is the joy-bringer: joy leads to self-expression and a search for law by which expressions may be controlled.
7. Law is the protector: knowledge of the law leads to courage.
8. Courage is the lifter: courage leads to trust.
9. Trust is the comforter: trust leads to truth.
10. Truth is the liberator: truth leads to freedom.
11. Freedom is the two-edged sword: freedom leads to opportunity.
12. Opportunity is the tester: opportunity rightly used leads to greatness.
13. Greatness is the witness: greatness leads to desire for further learning.
14. Learning is the path of the soul toward God: learning leads to wisdom.
15. Wisdom is the reward: wisdom leads to peace.
16. Peace is the life goal of earth man: peace leads to poise.
17. Poise is the stabilizer: poise leads to consciousness of the mind's creative power.
18. Creative power of the mind is the tempter of the soul of man. It leads to heaven or hell on earth according to whether it is used under love or outside of love. Right use of the creative power leads the individual soul to higher cosmic consciousness and, if continued, on to Christ consciousness.